TRAN...

FROM DARKNESS TO LIGHT

MW01135352

Transfigured: From Darkness to Light

Copyright © 2020 Charlie Shamp

All rights reserved. No part of this book may be used or reproduced by any means, graphic, electronic, mechanical, including photocopying, recording, taping, or by any information storage retrieval system without the written permission of the author except in the case of brief quotations embodied in critical articles and reviews.

For permissions beyond short quotations or if you have questions, please contact *Destiny Encounters International.*

https://www.destinyencounters.com/

Unless otherwise identified, Scripture quotations from The Authorized (King James) Version. Rights in the Authorized Version in the United Kingdom are vested in the Crown. Reproduced by permission of the Crown's patentee, Cambridge University Press Scripture quotations taken from the New American Standard Bible® (NASB), Copyright © 1960, 1962, 1963, 1968, 1971, 1972, 1973, 1975, 1977, 1995 by The Lockman Foundation. Scripture quotations marked "AMP" are taken from the Amplified® Bible, Copyright © 1954, 1958, 1962, 1964, 1965, 1987 by The Lockman Foundation. Scriptures taken from the Holy Bible, New International Version®, NIV®. Copyright © 1973, 1978, 1984, 2011 by Biblica, Inc.™ Used by permission of Zondervan. All rights reserved worldwide. www.zondervan.com The "NIV" and "New International Version" are trademarks registered in the United States Patent and Trademark Office by Biblica, Inc.™ Scripture quotations marked (NLT) are taken from the Holy Bible, New Living Translation, copyright ©1996, 2004, 2015 by Tyndale House Foundation. Used by permission of Tyndale House Publishers, a Division of Tyndale House Ministries, Carol Stream, Illinois 60188. All rights reserved. Scripture quotations are from the ESV® Bible (The Holy Bible, English Standard Version®), copyright © 2001 by Crossway, a publishing ministry of Good News Publishers. Used by permission. All rights reserved.

ISBN: 9798647507648

A Publication of Tall Pine Books

|| tallpinebooks.com

*Printed in the United States of America

TRANSFIGURED
FROM DARKNESS TO LIGHT

CHARLIE SHAMP

TALL PINE

CONTENTS

1 / EXTRACTING THE INVISIBLE

ABRAHAM HESCHEL, THE MASTER JEWISH THEOLOGIAN WHO SPECIALIZED in the Old Testament prophets, was a brilliant writer who created worlds with his words. An example of his exceptional gift was on display in 1972 during an interview on NBC, entitled "The Eternal Light." Here is one of the stimulating statements he made during that event: "*I see that the world itself is so fascinatingly mysterious, so challengingly marvelous, that there is more than I can see, that there is endlessly more than I can express or ever conceive.*"[1] On another occasion, Heschel spoke of the prophets as being "one octave too high for our ears." What was he trying to convey with these statements? I think that Heschel was indicating that the world is filled with enchanting enigmas and he was attracted to supernatural conundrums. In some ways, I believe that Heschel desired his own, one that would open his eyes to see the invisible. I am reasonably sure that his attraction to the heavenly dimensions were generated by his research and love for the prophets of God. The prophets lived in that invisible world and they were constantly manifesting the heavenly realm in the earthly sphere. I think he was quite sure that most people were not able to hear or see what the prophets of old faced. Faith is required!

Our faith is not fantasy. It seeks out and then adheres to the spiritual realities demonstrated in the time/space world, and beyond, going into the invisible world of spiritual realities. By faith we can extract the invisible and raise the level of our spiritual sight and hearing.

"By faith he forsook Egypt, not fearing the wrath of the king: for he endured, as seeing him who is invisible."[2] Moses, by faith, did not fear the wrath of the king and endured, as seeing Him who is invisible. Only faith can sustain us to live like Moses and encounter things in other dimensions, things that others consider unreal and impossible. Moses' faith gave him sight to grasp what others did not see. Faith allowed him to visit beyond the territory of the natural into the dominion of the supernatural. The invisible realities of the heavenly realm are visible to us through God's in-birthing of faith. In this hour, by faith, God wants us to understand how to take the invisible and make it become manifest, not just talking about some awesome revelation, but moving it into exhibition.

Before moving on, consider this. The Greek word for invisible is *aoratos* which means *invisible to the naked eye.* Millions of stars are invisible to us, however, they may be seen by a telescope. In the spiritual realm, there is much that is invisible to the naked eye, but it can be seen by heavenly technology. More to come!

GLORY REALMS OF ETERNITY

Ruth Ward Heflin, as a young girl, was carried by her parents to many of the healing revivalists like A.A. Allen and William Branham during the 1950's healing movement. Sister Ruth was well acquainted with the miraculous power of God. The insight God gave her brought freedom to countless thousands of Christians. The insight that changed everything were these words that came by revelation: "Praise until the Spirit of Worship comes, then worship until the glory comes, then stand in His glory." Sister Ruth had a great gift of opening doors into the glory realm for the Lord's people.

God actually put Himself in the glory realm of eternity, but He is bigger than eternity. In fact, He clothes Himself like a garment. "The LORD wraps himself in light as with a garment; he stretches out the heavens like a tent."[3] Augustine, while reflecting on eternity, wrote these words, "God's years, unlike ours, do not come and go. They are succeeded by no yesterday, and they give way to no tomorrow." Augustine continues on, "It is not in time that you precede all times, O Lord. You precede all pastimes and are the sublimity of an ever-present reality. You have made all times and are before all times. You are unchangeable and yet you change all things."[4] God covers the totality of every dimension and every universe. He has no beginning and no end, no parameters or margins or boundaries outside of God Himself.

You have an eternal sound on the inside of you that when you release it, the sound aligns yourself with the realm of glory, allowing you to be transported into that dimension, to receive the things that are invisible and then bring them back down to the earth. That's why the Bible says, "*Thy kingdom come. Thy will be done on earth, as it is in heaven.*"[5] All things start with the will of Father and it is certain that it is His will that all things be done on earth as it is in heaven. The challenge is to bring all things to earth as in heaven. This is the motto of the seekers: On earth as it is in heaven!

When you begin to worship and praise, you actually begin to create a vehicle of transportation that will assist you in bringing heaven to earth. Though your physical body never leaves the earth, your spiritual body is called to change worlds (just a teaser, more to come on that). Let me reiterate. The dimensions of the glory are all around us, but we need a vehicle through which we are transported that will carry us into a higher dimension where we are able to enter the supernatural world. Our eyes can be opened to everything that is around us, at all times. When you are in worship and praise, the spiritual dimension is opened and that which is invisible can become visible in the midst of God's people.

PRAY A MYSTERY

I find it sad that we can worship God, lifting up the name of Jesus, and begin to feel the atmosphere being saturated with the miraculous and yet never pull down anything out of the heavenly dimensions. We never harvest anything. The church must learn how to reap the things that we pray into.

Have you given much thought to this verse? *"For he that speaks in an unknown tongue speaks not to men, but to God: for no man understands him; however, in the spirit he speaks mysteries."*[6] First Corinthians 4:1 further enhances my point: *"Let a man so consider us, as servants of Christ and stewards of the mysteries of God."* Concerning the Greek word, *musterion,* Barnes Notes indicates that mystery is synonymous with sublime and elevated truth that was not before known, and that might be of the utmost importance.[7] *Strong's Concordance* and Vine's Expository Dictionary take a slightly different direction in their definition: "Mystery is that which denotes, not the mysterious (as with the English word), but that which, being outside the range of unassisted natural apprehension, can be made known only by Divine revelation, and is made known in a manner and at a time appointed by God, and to those only who are illuminated by His Spirit."[8] Summarizing Strong's and Vine's, it would be like this: Spiritual mysteries can only be made known by Divine revelation, at the appointed time, to those illuminated by the Spirit.

When you begin to pray in other tongues, you are praying mysteries—truths that have been made known to you by Divine revelation. You are beginning to "pray a mystery" to the Lord, and as you pray the mysteries, the prayers ascend into spiritual dimensions, creating an open heaven.

The mysteries that you are praying to the Lord clear the atmosphere and open the heavens, uncluttering the path so that the mystery comes back to you as an apocalypse, a revelation of a transcendent and preeminent truth that is of utmost importance. Have you ever prayed in this manner?

Paul's words are clear, *"...how that by revelation He made known to me the mystery."*[9] Paul was initiated "by revelation" into the mystery of God's divine purposes, not by his own reflective power, not by his exegesis of the Scripture, not by insights provided by other men, but by a special revelation from God generated by faith and steadfast pursuit of supernatural realities. His pursuit was so intense that heaven became attracted to the apostle.

You pray the mystery, and the mystery returns as a revelation of divine importance. The revelation brings manifestation. The invisible is unveiled the moment you receive the revelation. All you have to do is just take the invisible and bring it down into your world. That's how miracles happen. The church knows very little about extracting the invisible and how to cause the supernatural to come into the natural. So often, the people in the world are more successful than people in church and are more financially blessed. They have an abundance of inspired ideas that leads them to great wealth.

When we pray the mystery, it is converted into a revelation and the atmosphere becomes saturated with all kinds of possibilities, from miracles to creative concepts, all from the supernatural dimension. There is heavenly technology that God has brought into the atmosphere through our prayers, and someone that isn't even praying these things can simply grab them out of the atmosphere. They take these ideas and make millions of dollars off of them while the church sits around waiting for Jesus to come. Sorry for the taste of cynicism, but it is my desire to stir you up so that you do not miss the opportunities that are available to you as you pray the mystery.

These are special times and God wants us to learn how to take the invisible and divulge it to the world. We are about to see some of the most incredible advancements in technology than we have ever seen in any other generation. And that's because the church is going to tap into a greater dimension of the supernatural. It will happen as you enter that heavenly realm, a supernatural realm like the wheel within a wheel, riding on that chariot into another dimension, and enjoying the journey. Please tell me that you are getting excited about the possibilities that await us.

THE MIND OF CHRIST

In order to enter into this supernatural realm, it is imperative that your soul experience a spiritual metamorphosis, a transfiguration of your mind, in order that you would begin to think differently. *"And be not conformed to this world: but be ye transformed by the renewing of your mind."* [10]Be not conformed. Be ye transformed. As sons and daughters of the King, we are not to imitate or incorporate (external issues) the status and fashions of this transient world, but to be wholly transmuted (internal issue) in higher mode of thought, in strict accordance with God's revelatory desires. Barnes Notes offers this incredible perspective that will help clarify the importance of the renewing of the mind:

> "The word translated 'mind' properly denotes intellect, as distinguished from the will and affections. But here it seems to be used as applicable to the whole spirit as distinguished from the body, including the understanding, will, and affections. As if he had said, 'Let not this change appertain to the body only, but to the soul. Let it not be a mere external conformity, but let it have its seat in the spirit.' All external changes, if the mind was not changed, would be useless, or would be hypocrisy." [11]

I will take this to another level. When your soul begins to align itself in congruence with your spirit man, then what is joined to the spirit in perfect harmony will begin to manifest in your soul and body. Why do most Christians try to build up their spirit man, which has already been made perfect? *"To the general assembly and church of the firstborn, which are written in heaven, and to God the Judge of all, and to the spirits of just men made perfect."* [12] There is a company of theologians who believe that this refers to those made perfect and are in heaven already. However, there are those that believe that it also applies to those who still remain in this world. What is clear is that the just men are made perfect through Jesus the mediator of the new covenant, who worked out this perfect atonement through the shedding of the blood of Christ.

This might be a refresher course for those that don't remember. We human beings are complicated, as if you did not know. We are all very unique in the way we were created. However, God created all of us with the same three parts. The Bible tells us in 1 Thessalonians 5:23 that we were all created with three basic parts: a spirit, a soul, and a body.

> "And the God of peace Himself sanctify you wholly and may **your spirit and soul and body** be preserved complete, without blame, at the coming of our Lord Jesus Christ."

The body was created with the five senses in order to connect with the physical world. The soul is comprised of the mind, will, and emotion. The third part, and most powerful, is *the spirit*. The spirit is the deepest and most hidden part of our being. By our spirit we can contact the spiritual realm as we have written. Most theologians will say that the spirit is constituted by the deepest and most hidden part of our being. By our spirit we have communion with God and can have contact in His domain. The spirit is the preeminent part of man which joins him to God.

However, God wants to expand your soul so that you can begin to experience the other dimensions. Your physical body and soul are the parts of you that touch the earth, not your spirit. Your spirit is resting in heavenly places. Your soul is that which connects you to the earth. Actually, your soul causes the invisible to manifest because the soul is the middleman in between the spirit and the body. The renewed soul is now in a place where there can be more exposure to the supernatural realm.

When I tell people to put their hand on their mind, they obviously always put it on their brain. That's not your mind. Your brain is a muscle. Your mind is a partner with the spirit. But the mind and the spirit are connected. Paul offers these thoughts on the mind and the spirit: *"Those who live according to the flesh have their minds set on what the flesh desires; but those who live in accordance with the Spirit have their minds set on what the Spirit desires. The mind governed by the flesh is death, but the mind governed by the Spirit is life and peace."*[13]

When your mind is governed by the Spirit, it yields to the Spirit, and always minds the things of the Spirit. The mind is spiritual and becomes the mind of the Spirit. The mind, united with the Spirit, opens the door to the supernatural. The Spirit affects the mind so that they become one together. The mind, being in the Spirit, can contemplate and experience the supernatural. When the mind is brought under the influence of the Holy Spirit, the doors to other domains are opened. When the mind is of the things of the Spirit and under its influence, it is released into new dimensions of glory in the heavenly places.

When the mind of the soul is under the stimulus of the Spirit, it is like getting a new hard drive. In many respects, the hard drive is your computer. It is where all your data is stored and has the resources for the operating system, and it supplies what is needed to connect to the internet. In many ways, the mind is the interpreter of consciousness and for this reason it is indispensable that we maintain a mind renewed by the Spirit. God wants to keep your mind clean and pure so that it can run at maximum capacity and is not distracted by the world.

MULTI-DIMENSIONAL WORLDS

Nature consists of three dimensions: length, width, and height. We are not limited to these three; you will see that there are multiple dimensions. This 3-dimensional world includes flying through the atmosphere, descending into the depths of the ocean, or space travel to the ends of the earth.

I find this fascinating when we move deeper into the spiritual realm where we will encounter other dimensions. There is a blueprint in the heavenly realm that exhibits how to extract the supernatural and bring it into manifestation. Here is part of the challenge. I wonder whether the supernatural perception of too many people has atrophied. I would say that a major portion of the church has lost, if they ever had it, their passion and perception of the supernatural. It has been my desire for a long time to resurrect an understanding of the heavenly blueprint that will enable them to extract the supernatural and, by the power of the Holy Spirit, to experience other dimensions.

When God reveals to the church the deeper revelations of the supernatural domain and assists in the understanding of the blueprint of heaven, then we will be able to create whole new worlds. Scientists are discovering that we don't live in a universe. We live in a multiverse, a multidimensional world that awaits us. I know that, for many, it is difficult to comprehend what I am trying to unravel for you. I pray that you will open your heart to that which God wants to reveal to you. He longs for you to experience His presence in the divine dimensions of supernatural realities.

Mathematician Ian Stewart is accustomed to envisioning some pretty impossible shapes: snowflakes in fractional dimensions, hypercubes in 4-D, 11-dimensional superstrings. It was a super strange day for Stewart when he was introduced to Edwin A. Abbott's book entitled, *Flatland, A Romance of Many Dimensions*. The story revolves around a community of flatlanders who totally reject the concept of multiple dimensions. They are quite content with their boring little space of a two-dimensional world of flatlanders. It is Father's desire to liberate us from such small thinking and expose us to the multidimensionality of His creative work.

When God opens your eyes, you will see what you never saw before. The interaction between Jesus and Nicodemus must have been frustrating for the Master. Nicodemus was living in a 2-dimensional world like the flatlanders. Jesus starts the conversation with a download of intense revelation that will challenge his spiritual discernment: *"Jesus answered and said unto him, Verily, verily, I say unto thee, Except a man be born again, he cannot see the kingdom of God...Jesus answered, Verily, verily, I say unto thee, Except a man be born of water and of the Spirit, he cannot enter into the kingdom of God."*[14]

We are living in times where we are standing right now on holy ground and we are being required to make decisions concerning the direction we will take in the coming years. If you are to move into the spiritual dimensions that include *discerning heaven's blueprints and bringing heaven down to earth*, then you must be born again. You can't even see the kingdom until you're born again. This is more than making a profession of faith and getting baptized. This is not an altar call I am asking for. Unless you are born again, you cannot see the kingdom of God. Jesus expresses surprise, perhaps ironically, that Nicodemus, "a teacher of Israel," does not understand the concept of spiritual rebirth. Sometimes, you must be *born again... and again and again*.

Spiritual vision is dependent upon spiritual life. So, the spiritual vision which can see this kingdom is dependent upon spiritual life that is reflected by a radical change made possible by the inner working of the Holy Spirit. No external profession, no ceremonial observances or privileges of birth, could entitle any to the blessings of Messiah's kingdom. This heavenly birth is visibly reflected by a new nature, new principles, new affections, new aims, spiritual suscepti-bility, and receptiveness to the heavenly realm. This is not a worldly kingdom. It is of the heavenly realm and can only be perceived and discerned by the Spirit. Having been born again, a heavenly image has been stamped on your soul and you are now being called with a heavenly calling. This new life is brought about by a power from heaven. The spiritual realm of multiple dimensions awaits you.

> "If I have told you earthly things, and ye believe not, how shall ye believe if I tell you of heavenly things?"[15]

The earthly things are the elements of our 3-dimensional world that include the temporal things of this life. The heavenly things move from the known to the unknown. Barnes Notes describes the heavenly things in this way: "*They are things pertaining to the government of God and his doings in the heavens; things which are removed from human view, and which cannot be subjected to human sight.*" [16]The mysteries which are not of this world include much that you have never experienced but is opened to you: angelic encounters, heavenly transportations, and much more, which will be in the coming chapters.

When you are born again, the very first thing that opens is your spiritual eyes so that you begin to see into the spiritual multi-dimensions. Despite the natural limitations of the 3-dimensional world, there are other dimensions awaiting you.

In the glory, sound isn't just what we hear, it's what we see. Sound waves are not always invisible. Sound is simply the ordered vibration of matter. Any time you see a vibration, you see sound. Sound has a vibration that you can see. There are certain waves and frequencies of sound that can cause the invisible to become visible. *"When a jet flies close by over your house, you hear a rumble and see the silverware dance around on the table. That dancing motion is the sound waves from the jet traveling through your table and silverware."*[17]

Frequency is the number of complete oscillations per second of energy. All things in our universe are constantly in motion, vibrating. Even objects that appear to be stationary are in fact vibrating, oscillating, resonating, at various frequencies. Physicists are starting to come together around the notion that everything is created from some sort of vibrating energy.

It is certainly no mystery how the sound waves traveling down a guitar string are quite visible. When the words of a song are repeatedly heard within your mind, you can see the creative evidence of what is being played. This type of action has the potential to create something wonderful which looks like life, or something very dark that looks like death.

Sound waves and frequencies have the ability to touch something that is not visible to the naked eye, causing it to appear in plain view. This natural sound wave is known as sonar, a process critical to safe navigation in the ocean. Sonar is a method used for detecting and locating objects, especially underwater, by means of sound waves sent out to be reflected by the objects,

Sonar is simply the creation of an echo. When an animal or machine makes a noise, it sends sound waves into the environment around it. Those waves bounce off nearby objects, and some of them reflect back to the object that made the noise. The range of low-frequency sonar is remarkable.[18]

There is a sound that a piano cannot make. Guitars cannot make this sound. Drums cannot make this sound. Drums, guitars, and pianos were created simply for God's people to worship Him. In the beginning, God created you to worship Him and so there is an eternal sound that is in heaven's realm, at the very throne room of God.

The sound of heavenly vibrational frequency was put in you by God before the foundation of the earth. Humans have an optimal frequency, as does everything else in the universe. It occurs when each of the cells in our body vibrates at the frequency it was designed for. When you are in worship or praying in the Spirit, you can feel that vibration, a vibration created by God as a functioning part of the body. We are fearfully and wonderfully made.

In the early 1990s, Bruce Tainio, while working at Eastern State University in Cheney, Washington, built the world's first frequency monitor that could determine at exactly what vibration the human body most often oscillates.[19] Taino found that a healthy body resonates at a frequency of 62-70 MHz, and when your frequency drops to 58 MHz, that is when disease starts.[20] There are positive and negative things that will impact our inner frequency (designed by God), such as faith and hope or doubt and fear.

DIVINE ENERGY

In the beginning, you were part of the eternal realm for your spirit was with Him. You were there before you ever came here. That's why when you show up there, it feels like you're at home. How did you get here? *"And the Lord God formed man of the dust of the ground and breathed into his nostrils the breath of life; and man became a living soul."*[21]

"And the Lord God formed man..." The metaphor is that of the potter shaping and molding clay. He is made not from the rocks, nor from ores of metal, but from the light, shifting particles of the surface, blown about by every wind. Yet, frail as is man's body.[22]

The preceding clause explains man's bodily structure and the present one explains the origin of his life. His life is not the product of his body, but the gift of God's breath or spirit. The prophetic thought in this section of the Pulpit Commentary is powerful:

> "The origin of their soul was coincident with that of their corporeality (the body), and their life was merely the individualization of the universal life with which all matter was filled at the beginning by the Spirit of God."

Genesis 2:7 KJV says, "*...and breathed into his nostrils the breath of life; and man became a living soul.*" God breathed into man. By the magnitude of His power and through the direction of Divine force and the vibrational frequency in the lung, the Ruach Elohim is pushed with pulsating energy through the nose, circulating back through the lung and the chest wall until it flows through the mouth and man comes to life. The lifeless lump of clay is quickened by the spirit. "*Man received his life from a distinct act of Divine inbreathing; certainly not an inbreathing of atmospheric air, but an inflatus from the Ruach Elohim, or Spirit of God, a communication from the whole personality of the Godhead.*"[23]

When Adam was designed and until the moment of his sin, he was a fusion of heaven and earth (dimensionally speaking). In the Garden of Eden, he walked with God, who inhabits eternity. "*For thus says the High and Lofty One Who inhabits eternity, whose name is Holy:*"[24] "While living in the Garden of Eden, Adam experienced the multi-dimensions of eternity, but he also lived in the earthly zone of space/time."[25] Man was made for eternity and though he lost that life in the dimension of eternity, it is recovered through the blood of Christ.

SONAR ECHO

Before there was darkness or light, time or space, there was stillness. In the stillness of the moment, a sound breaks through. "*And God said...*" When God breathed into man, He breathed into man the sound, the eternal sound, the sound of heaven. You're resting in the created universe, and within is an eternal sound wanting you to release it. God desires to release a sound through us, a sound that will shake the earth.

Indeed, there is a sound from heaven. It is the sound of a divine convergence between heaven and earth. It is like an echo. When you're releasing the sound from you, it's like a sonar echo that's going out and returning back to its original source. That spiritual vibration is being released and as it's released, suddenly you're able to begin to see the things that are invisible. In that moment, the Spirit and your voice are lifted toward God. The sonar echo is returning back to its original source and suddenly your eyes see your miracle. It's coming closer to you. Beep, beep, beep.

The divine alignment, created by the sonar echo, allows you to be transported into that eternal dimension, to receive and experience the things in invisible places. The moment is now right to bring them back down to the earth. As I have written, that's why the Bible says *as it is in heaven, so shall it be on the earth;* but God needs you to release it yourself. That's why worship connects you to that realm. Open your mouth in praise. Free your spirit to worship, a divine exchange between heaven and earth. He releases the sounds, you respond. He moves, you move. You are a spirit and He has called you to worship Him in spirit and in truth. Your spirit and your body resonate with the sound. The more that you spend time worshiping and praising the Lord, you're actually creating a throne of His presence, or the eye of God, over your life. A transportation device is uniquely created for you to carry you into another dimension.

Sonar is similar to worship. When an instrument is played or a song is sung, a frequency or a wave is released into the realm of the spirit where many things exist but are not visible to the naked eye. When this sound penetrates the spirit realm, it causes the invisible to become visible. The Lord has begun to reveal a generation on the earth that has sounded the sonar and they will carry the frequency, the vibration of the spirit, and they will release heaven's frequency

LIGHT AND SOUND

Sound and light are similar in that both are forms of energy that travel in waves. They both have properties of wavelength, frequency, and amplitude. The waves of sound or light both reflect, refract, and attenuate depending on their environment. Sound is like light in these ways: it travels out from a definite source (such as an instrument or a noisy machine), just as light travels out from the Sun or a light bulb. But there are great differences between light and sound.[26]

Sound waves travel a million times slower than light waves. They have wavelengths between 1 centimeter and 10 meters and will easily diffract around corners. Light waves have much smaller wavelengths, and only diffract through very small holes. This difference is the reason why you can often hear things that you cannot see.[27]

There are some Jewish scholars who believe that when God said *let there be light*, that it was actually a *song* that He released. He actually began to sing over all of creation. Light and sound combined together to sing to the glory of God.

Ray Hughes described it this way: "Essentially, we know that these categories and forms of light and sound fall within the same spectrum. The first time God said, 'Let there be light' (Genesis 1:3), He was also proclaiming the beginning of sound."[28]

Hughes adds one more thought to his concept regarding 'our unique sound': "Christ will be revealed as we hear His sound and release our individual, God-appointed sound as His unique instruments. '...Christ in you, the hope of glory' (Colossians 1:27). The word *glory* means *lightified*. From this, we can deduce that Christ in you is the hope of being *lit,* or the hope of being *sounded*. Christ is your hope of producing the sound that has resided in you since the beginning of time. Your sole purpose of existence as a worshiper of God is to be the personal instrument He created you to be, and to be played for His glory. With the very truth of the living Christ is the assurance you will be played before God."

GENETIC CODE

All of creation is eagerly waiting and moaning and groaning for the manifestation of the sons of God.[29] The Arabic interpreter puts the word *glory* into the text, and reads the word thus: "*The earnest expectation of the creature waiteth for the manifestation of the glory of the sons of God:*"[30] Their glory for the present was hidden, but it shall be discovered and manifested as heavenly waves are released and miracles happen. There's a frequency that can only be released to His sons and His daughters.

By nature of creation and an internal and an eternal sound, we are tied to both the earth and to the heavenly realm. We are connected to our creation where the Creator formed man from the earth. We are bonded to the Savior's blood that was shed at Golgotha. The Word who created man is the same Word who saved man. You have been waiting. The results of your blood tests are here. Your DNA proves that you are related to Christ by His blood. In fact, the whole world was created upon the blood of Jesus. The Bible says that before the foundation of the earth, Christ was the slain Lamb (Revelation 13:8). That means that the DNA of the earth holds the genetic code, which contains the Blood of Jesus.

The Hebrew word 'man' is the word *adamah*. The word *adamah* could be more literally translated "red ground," and the name *Adam*, could be said to mean "red man."[31] That means there's a close association between the spirit of man and the physical earth of the ground. The genetic code of the supernatural connects humans to heaven and to earth. That's why God said "you will have dominion over the earth."

The cells and the DNA have a vibration, a frequency on the inside of them. Your genetic code, when it's in proper alignment, is able to tap into both dimensions, heaven and earth. That's why Paul by inspiration of the Holy Spirit said, "*Do you not know that you are the temple of God and that the Spirit of God dwells in you?*"[32]

Consider this verse in 1 Kings 8:27: "*But will God indeed dwell on the earth? Behold, heaven and the heaven of heavens cannot contain You.*" In a sense, your physical body is greater than the whole entire universe. Let that sink in before moving on.

You contain this heavenly transportation device, not just in the ARK but in the A-R-C, the arc, the path above and below celestial bodies. When the arc, the vibration, the frequency, are in alignment with your spirit, your soul, and your body, then you are able to create that perfect sound that brings you into that spiritual dimension. And when you're in that realm, all things are possible.

Some people think your body is evil, but God created your body in alignment with your genetic code and therefore you should never die. Your cells should reproduce after themselves without complications. It doesn't make any sense why the physical body should die. Yet, because of sin, Adam's gene cells were affected and, unfortunately, he was expelled from Eden's garden and all creation suffered the consequences.

But when man is born again, there is a genetic restructuring of spirit, soul, and body. Though guilty, my sin has been atoned for. By faith, I can experience all that God desired for me because of what Jesus has done and suffered for me. Jesus has done all that God required and I am free from condemnation, and I must now live for Him. Your genetic code is repaired, and your life has dramatically changed. The old man is gone and the new man lives. Nothing more remains to be done. You cannot add to perfection. What more can *we* do, when *God* says, "I am *satisfied*." He has sent down the Holy Spirit as a sign of His forgiveness.

Let's get back to the genetic code. A DNA molecule consists of two strands wound around each other, with each strand held together by bonds between the bases. Genetic code is the term we use for the way that the four bases of DNA (the A, C, G, T) are strung together. The sequence of bases in a portion of a DNA molecule, called a gene, carries the instructions needed to assemble a protein.[33] Think of it this way. We have the potential of being gene carriers, traveling into new dimensions where revelation is received and delivered to God's people.

There is another way to describe the genetic code. Jesus was quite impressed with young Nathaniel, so impressed that He delivered these amazing words to this new disciple: *"Then he said, 'I tell you the truth, you will all see heaven open and the angels of God going up and down on the Son of Man, the one who is the stairway between heaven and earth.'"*[34] Whether it is a gene carrier or a supernatural ladder, it is God's purpose that we ascend into spiritual dimensions and see things we have never seen and hear things we have never heard. Then the time will come to descend and bring them back into the earthly dimension. It is inevitable for you to experience the heavenly realms of glory. Your internal genetic code connects you to that dimension. Because of your DNA, your genetic code, you were meant to be a worshipper, a glory carrier, and a traveler into the heavenly realms.

"That the God of our Lord Jesus Christ, the Father of glory, may give unto you the spirit of wisdom and revelation in the knowledge of him:"[1]

AT THE AGE OF THIRTEEN, A YOUNG JEWISH BOY BECOMES RESPONSIBLE for his conduct. This milestone in his life is celebrated by an event called a bar mitzvah. The Jewish people believe that at this time something dramatic happens to their mind, "a sort of awakening, a state of consciousness, a realization that 'I exist.' The Jewish sages called it da'at—roughly translated as 'knowledge' or 'consciousness.' Knowledge usually means knowledge about things outside of oneself. But this da'at is the knowledge of the one who is knowing the "I."[2]

There is nothing more frightening than knowledge of Jehovah, but as children of God, there is nothing more empowering and stimulating than knowing and encountering God. Knowledge is not to be minimized, as addressed below by the prophet Hosea.

"*My people are destroyed for lack of knowledge: because you have rejected knowledge, I will also reject you, that you shall be no priest to me: seeing you have forgotten the law of your God, I will also forget your children.*"[3] The destruction is in the deception, deceived because of their lack of knowledge and by listening to the voice of false teachers. They accepted pseudo knowledge in exchange for the true knowledge of God.

Barnes Notes composes these words as he inscribed with a pen the danger of the privation of knowledge by saint and preacher. "The true knowledge of God is the life of the soul, true life, eternal life, as our Savior saith, 'This is life eternal, that they should know Thee, the only true God, and Jesus Christ whom Thou hast sent.' The source of this lack of knowledge, so fatal to the people, was the willful rejection of that knowledge by the priest."[4]

"For the earth shall be filled with the knowledge of the glory of the LORD, as the waters cover the sea."[5] The glory of the Lord will be unveiled at the destruction of His enemies and the restoration and revelation of the true knowledge of God. The glory of Christ will transcend any earthly glory, which is a false glory. The knowledge of the glory gives you access to understand how to operate in the glory. There's a difference.

I understand that the glory is *available*, but it isn't available until I have *the knowledge of it*. With knowledge comes greater understanding and we learn how to receive and function in the glory. A world full of the knowledge of God's glory brings joy and excitement. Where there is an abundance of the knowledge of His glory, the unlearned and ignorant become wise and eloquent, the earthly become heavenly, and the deceived become enlightened. This is the power of growing in knowledge.

In the late second century's *Letter to Dionetus*, the unknown author wrote these words concerning knowledge: "What we live in and enjoy of what God has provided is limited by our knowledge of it. We can only live in what we know. We can only prosper to the degree our souls prosper. We can only live in the perfect will of God to the degree our minds are renewed to know it and apply it. We can live like God only to the degree that we THINK like God. But he who combines knowledge with fear, and seeks after life, plants in hope, looking for fruit. Let your heart be your wisdom; and let your life be true knowledge inwardly received."[6] We can live like God only to the degree that we THINK like God.

I can know that there's a car outside and it has keys. I can know that the car is available for me, but if I don't know how to start the car, or how to put it in drive and drive the car, then I'm not leaving the parking lot. And if I do leave the parking lot, I'm going to get pulled over because I don't know any of the laws.

The knowledge of God is like a treasure chest buried deep in the earth. It is there for you, but you must be willing to get the shovel and start digging. Like Jesus said, *"Ask, and it shall be given you; seek, and ye shall find; knock, and it shall be opened unto you."*

So, God wants to teach us how to move in His glory. *"Each new day brings more of the story. The heavens tell about the glory of God. The skies announce what his hands have made. Each new day tells more of the story, and each night reveals more and more about God's power."*[7] The heavens have a story to tell. It is the story of God's glory. Every day there is more to learn. Knowledge is essential. Knowledge is necessary because it is a key to discernment and decisions. The great men and women of the past focused on prayer and the pursuit of revelation knowledge. Knowledge brings light.

Fiat lux...let there be light! We reflect the light which shines upon us from the divine glory. Reflected light will guide us to blueprints and keys, and to the discovery and demonstration of the glory. *"For God, who commanded the light to shine out of darkness, has shined in our hearts, to give the light of the knowledge of the glory of God in the face of Jesus Christ."*[8]

God, the Creator of light, conferred upon us the light that shone out of darkness. It is this same light that shines into our hearts giving us, His saints, knowledge and insight into the glory.

What we have received concerning the glory of God, we freely give to others. God makes use of us in spreading the news of the glory. It is our purpose to bring others to see the fellowship of this mystery, the glory of God, all which is made possible "in the face of Jesus Christ."

"And he shewed me a pure river of water of life, clear as crystal, proceeding out of the throne of God and of the Lamb. In the midst of the street of it, and on either side of the river, was there the tree of life, which bore twelve manner of fruits, and yielded her fruit every month: and the leaves of the tree were for the healing of the nations."[9]

One of the peculiar contradictions is the fact that Jerusalem was not built by a river. The Jews always anticipated that one day the Holy City, like the great cities of the world, would have a river. The prophets dreamed and would sing of a river. On one occasion, Ezekiel dreamed of a river rushing out of Jerusalem. Isaiah, in a prophetic vision, saw a future Jerusalem where he says, *"There the Lord will be our Mighty One. It will be like a place of broad rivers and streams."*[10] In the heart of the Jews, there is a desire for a river by the perfect city. The Psalmist believed that God resided by the rivers of heaven. *"There is a river whose streams make glad the city of God, the holy habitation of the Most High."*[11]

Before moving on, let's consider the importance of water. Water is an essential nutrient and plays a key role in the human body. We can survive up to several weeks without food, but only a few days without water. Every system in the body, from cells and tissues, to vital organs requires water to function. "Water carries nutrients to all cells in our body and oxygen to our brain. Water allows the body to absorb and assimilate minerals, vitamins, amino acids, glucose and other substances. Water flushes out toxins and waste. Water helps to regulate body temperature. Water acts as a lubricant for joints and muscles."[12] All creation is drawn to rivers and oceans. Beside the river, we are strengthened and stimulated. In that contemplative place, we are drawn to higher realms beyond the mundane world we live in. *"There is a river whose streams make glad the city of God, The holy dwelling places of the Most High."*[13] Far away from the troubled places in the world around us, we are taken to a place of peace and joy. Sitting on the banks of the river, we rejoice to be in the presence of Mighty God, our lover and our friend.

There are two important references to 'rivers' in the Bible. One is in Genesis and the other is in Revelation. Genesis 2:10-14 tells us that a river went out of Eden to water the garden, and that it parted and became four rivers: the Pishon, Gihon, Hiddekel, and Euphrates. Now consider this verse in the light of the rivers in Genesis. *"For we are God's fellow workers [His servants working together]; you are God's culti-vated field [His garden, His vineyard], God's building."*[14]

The rivers of God were created for the watering of the garden, which are the people of God. The heavens of river are for the life of the believer.

"And he shewed me a pure river of water of life, clear as crystal, proceeding out of the throne of God and of the Lamb. In the midst of the street of it, and on either side of the river, was there the tree of life, which bore twelve manner of fruits, and yielded her fruit every month: and the leaves of the tree were for the healing of the nations."[15] It is the pure stream, the crystal stream that flows out of the throne of God and the Lamb. The stream flows through the city and parallel to the river of life are streets in the midst of which are trees of life and the trees of healing; healing for the nations. Most theologians agree that there are multiple trees rather than one tree as in the Garden of Eden.

When the *Heaven of Rivers* flows through a meeting, you'll start to feel like the waters are rising. It is like the man in the book of Ezekiel where an angel led Ezekiel into the water until it reached his ankles, then his loins, and then till he was able to swim in the waters. How many have ever felt that way before? That's a river of healing that begins to flow in the meeting and miracles start happening, and people get blessed. Like we have just read, this river flows straight from the throne of God. The Heaven of Rivers is for the growth of God's garden, His people. The Heaven of Rivers in Revelation combined with the tree of life is to produce life and are for the healing of the nations.

God wants life to flow through you. He wants to touch every part of your life. He wants to touch every situation that you are facing. He wants to reverse every curse you sense. He wants to bring you out of depression and into supernatural joy. He wants to heal your body and keep you healed. In John 7:38 Jesus says, *"He that believeth on me, as the scripture hath said, out of his belly shall flow rivers of living water."*

Rivers are going to flow out of you. Streams and tributaries will flow through you and around you. It is going to bless you and it's going to bless everybody around you. We are the river of God that will bring life and healing to those around us and to the nations.

HEAVEN OF LIGHTS

"Now it happened, as I journeyed and came near Damascus at about noon, suddenly a great light from heaven shone around me."[16]

These words were declared by Paul from his narrative during the trial before the Sanhedrin at Jerusalem. You know the story. Saul had left Jerusalem and headed to Damascus, traveling along the Roman Road. He has one purpose. Kill the Christians! The big event happens shortly before arriving in Damascus.

At midday a great 'light from heaven,' brighter than the noonday sun, exploded in Saul's presence. It makes one wonder how near to us the unseen world is! It is in any moment that God can draw aside the veil and heaven will appear. This was no flash of lightning. It was the light of heaven and the glory of Christ shining directly into the face of Saul, causing him to collapse.

It seems that Jesus appeared to check out Saul's persecuting zeal. The glory of this heaven-sent light should not be confounded with any natural phenomenon. It was in the midst of heaven's glory that Christ was seen by Saul. "Some have thought that Saul, being a learned Jew, would easily know this to be the *Shekinah,* or visible token of the divine presence. I think that he did understand this since he cried out, *"Who art thou, Lord?"*

[17]This is a very short conversation. Jesus tells Saul that He is

Jesus, "the One you are persecuting." *Uh, oh! Not good.* Saul then replies and asks Jesus what he should do. *Big change of heart!* Jesus tells him, "Go to the city and it will be shown to you what to do."

In the eruption of a moment, Saul's firm conviction against the gospel and his unwearied persecutions are suddenly and radically changed. It all started with the Heaven of Lights.

It is in the realm of the Heaven of Lights that you begin to see signs, wonders, miracles, and divine manifestations. I was in a meeting in Orlando, Florida, and the sun was so bright in the meeting. I kept going, could not stop, because we hit that realm in heaven and the Spirit was lighting up the room. However, it was brutal, because the sun shining in from outside was directly in my eyes. Some people knew what was happening, and others were looking at me and wondering, "Why is he squinting and looking funny?"

Have you ever been in a meeting where you got a suntan? I've been in meetings where people got suntans. I was in California and a lady got a suntan in my meeting. In every meeting, she was getting darker and darker and darker.

In this meeting, people started going into the sun, into that light. And there was a man sitting in the front row, and his hair was speckled white and black. But, as he stayed longer in the sun, his head must have felt like a bonfire. It was burning and had started changing back to black. Right in front of the people, they're screaming and pointing and taking pictures as it was going back to black. I asked him, "What does it feel like?" He replied, "I feel like my head is on fire. It's burning like I'm being touched by the sun."

We reached a higher realm. It's called Heaven of the Throne. This is where you are in the very Throne Room of God. This is where I like to be.

CLOTHED WITH A ROBE

"And I will clothe him with thy robe, and strengthen him with thy girdle, and I will commit thy government into his hand: and he shall be a father to the inhabitants of Jerusalem, and to the house of Judah. And the key of the house of David will I lay upon his shoulder; so he shall open, and none shall shut; and he shall shut, and none shall open. And I will fasten him as a nail in a sure place; and he shall be for a glorious throne to his father's house."[18]

"The son of Hilkiah who succeeded Shebna as governor of the palace and 'grand vizier' (a high-ranking political advisor, similar to Joseph's position under Pharaoh) under Hezekiah. The functions of his office are seen from the oracle of Isaiah in which Shebna is deposed and Eliakim set in his place. At his installation he is clothed with a robe and girdle, the insignia of his office, and, having the government committed into his hand, is the father to the inhabitants of Jerusalem, and to the house of Judah. The key of the house of David is laid on his shoulder, and he alone has power to open and shut, this being symbolic of his absolute authority as the king's representative."[19]

According to Bible history, the 'sash' or girdle was perhaps the most beautiful figurative mode of expression used for clothing among the prophets. The girdle was wound several times around the waist to bind the clothing together. This essentially means that as the girdle has a controlling and binding influence over all of the bodily attire, so these qualities have a controlling and binding influence over all of His purposes and actions.[20]

Recently I had a dream, or a night vision, and during the dream I went into the realm of the Spirit. I was taken into the tabernacle. I've been there a few times in heaven. The Lord brought me there because He wanted to show me a specific thing about the robe. I saw the priests. But more importantly, I saw the Melchizedek priesthood.

I saw some people that were there that are on the earth now, and I knew that they were part of this order. In fact, everyone in the dream was part of this order. Moreso, everybody that is in the body of Christ has been called to be a part of this order. This is not the Levitical priesthood, for that is part of the old. The new order is the *order of Melchizedek.*

I won't address much concerning Melchizedek, but I will touch on a few things to give perspective to my point. Melchizedek appears in the books of Genesis and Hebrews. Melchizedek, in Hebrew, means 'king of righteousness.' He is the king of Salem, which in the Hebrew root, means *peace*. He is the king of righteousness whose kingdom is a kingdom of peace. After Lot's liberation from a band of Mesopotamian kings, Melchizedek shows up in Abraham's camp and shares bread and wine with him and then speaks a blessing over Abraham.

I'll close this section on Melchizedek with these key verses from Psalms and Hebrews. In Psalm 110:4, the psalmist declares, "*You are a priest forever, in the order of Melchizedek.*"

I follow up with these words in Hebrews 5:5-6, "*So also Christ glorified not himself to be made an high priest; but he that said unto him, Thou art my Son, today have I begotten thee. As he saith also in another place, Thou art a priest forever after the order of Melchizedek.*"

This is the summary note. The law required that all priests be of the tribe of Levi and Jesus was from the tribe of Judah, not from the tribe of Levi. Melchizedek is a type of Christ, because Jesus is a priest, but not of the Levitical order. "*He does not do His work inside the earthly tabernacle, but He does it in the heavenly realities. Why? He's a priest of a different order, an eternal order, one that has no beginning or no end.*"[21] Don't forget these words: **He does not do His work inside the tabernacle, but He does it in the heavenly realities.**

You are ordained of the order of Melchizedek and God wants you to operate as kings and priests. In the final moments of the dream, there was a transition. The Lord brought me there, and an angel was there with me, and I don't want to focus on the angel, but I just want to share that the angel was speaking to me, and he showed me a garment that was on one of their priests.

I said to the angel that brought me there, "What is that garment?" I was curious about the garment. It was like a translucent robe that the priest was wearing. So I said, "Lord, what is that?" He replied, "That's the robe of invincibility."" Every priest and king has this robe. The Lord spoke to me and said, "Now you've operated with that robe in the past without knowing it, but I want to teach it to you. I want to show you it so that you can begin to talk to people in the body of Christ about activating this robe." There is a robe that you have been given.

I came out of this encounter and I said, "Lord, the priests didn't wear a robe." But I want you to consider this verse, Exodus 28:2, 4: *"And thou shalt make holy garments for Aaron thy brother for glory and for beauty. And they shall make holy garments for Aaron thy brother, and his sons, that he may minister unto me in the priest's office."*

This robe was given to Aaron and the Levitical priesthood, sons of Levi, and the robes were exclusively for this earthly priesthood, not for the people. There is another robe that is a heavenly robe that is given to all those that are new creations in Christ. You are from the order of Melchizedek, ministers in the heavenly place and called to possess the garment.

ENCOUNTER, THEN STUDY

This happens to me regularly. I'll first see something dramatic in the realm of the Spirit, and then I'll go and study it. I have noticed that people like to study it first and then try to have the encounter. But, that's not the way God operates. Most people will first have the encounter, the experience, and then it will take you months to unravel that thing. After the experience, my mind and spirit are in total recall, trying to figure out what happened. "What is this? I have never seen this before. I've never heard this talk before. No one has ever taught me this. So, it's not like I could learn this from a book." I couldn't just pick up somebody's book and say, "Yeah, there's the cloak of invisibility and invincibility. That sounds fascinating. I think I'm going to go and teach on that."

That's what some people like to do. They just go and gather information and then regurgitate it back to the people. That's not what God wants. It is my thought that God is looking for those whose revelations are built on a platform of personal encounters with God and experiences in the supernatural realm. He wants to first allow us to have an encounter with Him and then, out of that encounter, revelation begins to come.

I'll add a little more to the mystery. In Bible Study Tools, they offer a good perspective on mystery. *Musterion*, the Greek word for mystery, in the Bible means those truths which are part of God's plan and can only be understood as He reveals them by His Spirit and through His Word. Stated another way, *musterion* is "a secret purpose of God which when uncovered is understood by the Spirit-taught believer."[22]

It refers to a truth which without special revelation would have been unknown. The mystery then becomes *apocalypto,* which is the word *revelation.* So, then the thing that is hidden suddenly becomes uncovered, so then you have understanding about it. With revelation comes the ability to move and operate in the revealed truth.

If you don't know what's available, then you don't know how to move in it. You don't even know it's accessible to you, unless you stumble into it. But this is not the way.

Paul was a brilliant man, trained through the formal education of the most prominent rabbinical schools of that day. Among his teachers, young Saul had the privilege to be trained by Gamaliel, the most outstanding rabbi of that time. Gamaliel was one of the most honorable and reputable Jewish rabbis during the days of the apostles. He was the grandson of Hillel, the founder of the most influential rabbinical school of Judaism; Gamaliel was also the president of the Sanhedrin in succession of his father. It was in this environment that Saul received his education in the religion of Judaism and became well versed in its dogma and apologetics.[23] However, Paul went through a major reconstruction of his life. His new teacher was the Holy Spirit. Revelation is not something of the mind, it is of the Spirit, as indicated in Paul's letter below to the Corinthians. His teacher was once the great Gamaliel, but now his teacher was the Holy Spirit who taught him how to combine spiritual thoughts with spiritual words.

"Now we have received, not the spirit of the world, but the Spirit who is from God, so that we may know the things freely given to us by God, which things we also speak, not in words taught by human wisdom, but in those taught by the Spirit, combining spiritual thoughts with spiritual words."[24]

ROBE OF INVISIBILITY AND INVINCIBILITY

This garment is a clear, translucent garment that allows you to move through the earth, unseen. You can step into places and begin to see things that are taking place in governments and in dark conspiratorial places. God does not give you those experiences to exalt you, but so that you can move into intercession in a higher dimension and take it into the heavenly courts, so that the particular issue will be judged on the earth.

Now, I have to be a little bit careful because there are some places in this world that are incredibly dangerous, and wisdom and spiritual insight must be exercised. I know that there are some people in the body of Christ who have tried to move into this dimension without using this garment. There have been some who were severely attacked even; some of them have been overcome by warfare attacks that have come against them. This is not for the immature, nor the unprepared.

They thought the enemy was coming against them, but actually what was taking place was that there were some people moving out of another spirit that saw you there. Quickly, they tried to attack you because they were sent by demonic assignment to keep you out of that place, so you do not gain access to this critical information.

The Lord said that as you begin to move with this garment, they will not be able to see you. And you'll be able to go into that place, discern what is happening, and be able to reverse curses and switch things around. It is amazing what can be done if you are protected by the robe of a garment.

When you begin to operate out of righteousness, you begin to operate out of invincibility, and you operate out of clarity. You will be able to go into places and see things in the realm of the Spirit. People won't be able to discern that you are there yet, but you are in their presence in that place, hearing the conversations that they are having. At that point, you must exercise discernment and make sure you are judging righteously in those situations so you can change them.

Here is another important truth: most people do intercession from earth to heaven, but God called you to do it from heaven to the earth. The Bible says, *"For in him we live, and move, and have our being;"*[25] The words 'In Christ' became Paul's constant theme to the Gentile churches, especially the church at Ephesus.

In fact, that phrase is mentioned 134 times. No words can better convey our continuous dependence on God. In Christ we have received redemption through His blood, the forgiveness of sins, the riches of His grace, and the gift of wisdom, and He has made known unto us the mystery of His will. There is no idea of dependence more striking than the fact that we can make the slightest motion and it is because of Christ. We are united to Christ the Vine and receive our nourishment and support from Him.

On the inside of Christ, that is where you are at, on the inside of Him. The Bible says that you're seated with Christ in heavenly places. You are seated on the inside. You are on the inside of that throne. You're on the inside of that kingdom. You're on the inside of that power. You're on the inside of that presence. And when you are inside of Him, then you can move beyond an earthly dimension. You can move here and there throughout the earth because "in Him I live and move and have my being."

Because I am in Christ, I can be in multiple places at one time. That means I could be preaching to you right now and be somewhere completely different because I'm not operating out of myself. I am now operating out of Christ. When you begin to operate out of the Genetic Code and wear the divine garment, you move into realms you never expected. You are operating out of the blessings of both king and priest.

REALM OF MAR'EH

I have this feeling that while some of you are reading this stuff about the garment of invisibility, you might be thinking I have lost my marbles. I am thinking that I need some scriptural confirmation. I remember thinking about this and then speaking out, "Lord, give me three scriptures that will demonstrate the truth of what I am teaching, and this way, people won't think that I am a bit wild and crazy." I told the Lord if He doesn't show me three verses in the Bible that confirm what I am teaching, then I will never preach it again. That's what I told Him. I said, "Lord, nobody will believe me. They'll think that I'm not preaching the Bible," because people believe in Father, Son, and Holy Bible.

I repeat, "Lord, give me three scriptures on it. Show me three scriptures." Well, I received the first scripture. *"And, behold, the angel of the Lord came upon him, and a light shone in the prison: and he smote Peter on the side, and raised him up, saying, Arise up quickly. And his chains fell off from his hands. And the angel said unto him, Gird thyself, and bind on thy sandals. And so he did. And he saith unto him, Cast thy garment about thee, and follow me"* [26]

Cast your garment, the garment of invisibility, upon you and follow Me. King Herod was prepared to crush the life out of the Christians. First, he killed James, the brother of John, and then he had Peter thrown in prison. Peter was in the inner dungeon and expecting that at some point his life would be taken also. This is NOT what he expected. An angel came to him in the middle of the night. Peter thinks that he is in vision mode. The angel shakes him, awakens him, and then says, "Gird thyself up, put thy sandals on, and put this cloak on."

Some people think that this cloak was a natural cloak, but that was actually a heavenly garment that was given to Peter. He put the cloak on, became 'invisible man' and walked through the prison without ever being seen. He thought that he was in a *Chazon*, the Hebrew word for *dream*, but he was actually in *Ma'reh*, the Hebrew word for *appearances or visions.* Moses had a similar experience at the burning bush as Peter had in the Roman prison.

And Moses saith, 'Let me turn aside, I pray thee, and I see this great appearance; wherefore is the bush not burned?' Ma'reh is a place where you are walking along a strange path and the heavenly realm becomes more real than the natural world. That is the Ma'reh realm that Peter entered into.

Following the angel, Peter was covered with the cloak and was unable to be seen by any guards. He walked through that place, thinking he was in a vision, but when he finally got to the outer place, past all of the opened doors, he knew that this was a supernatural event.

He was able to go through the jail and when he got to the other side, suddenly his eyes were open to realize that he was not in a visionary realm in the dungeon. Now he's on the outside because he was clothed with a spiritual garment that protected him with a cloak of invisibility.

There's going to come a time when you will be able to move in this dimension of the invisible garment. You will go into places and they won't be able to see you. You will minister in nations that are closed and they will want to kill you. However, when they seek to find you, they won't be able to, because you understand how to operate out of an invisibility garment. Governments will try to come and take you, but they won't be able to find you.

Several years ago, I was in Brazil, and I was ministering in the capital city of Brasilia. I was talking to some guys that went with me to minister in the city. Suddenly, I said, "Guys," and we just started talking about Enoch. When you start to stir up people's testimony, suddenly the testimony will come on you. So, I said, "Guys, I feel like I'm expanding right now. I feel like something's happening, like I'm going into a different dimension. I feel like I'm expanding." We were just talking about Enoch and thinking that something amazing was happening. I look at the guys and say, "Something's happening, guys. Something is just taking place right now."

This is when the Lord first started to stir this thing up. I didn't know what it was, but I was just following, just trusting Him because something was happening. I feel like I'm expanding, like something's coming on me. I couldn't stop and try and figure this out. We had to go meet our host, and in this city, many of the buildings have armed guards and the doors are closed, so that bad people can't get in.

This guy lived in one of those buildings like I described, and he lives on the 12th floor of this building. The guards are standing outside and I just walk up to the door. The guards are standing there. I just open up the door and all the guys follow me. We get on the elevator, we go to the 12th floor, and we knock on the door. The guy goes, "Who's there?" I said, "Hey, it's me, Charlie." He opens up the door. He says, "How did you get in?"

I told him that I just walked over to the door, opened it, and walked straight through. He said, "Impossible... that's *impossible.*" He went on to say, "I would have rung the bell so the guards would let you in." I said, "Well, I just walked through." The owner calls down to the guards. "Hey, did you see these guys come in?" They said, "No, no one's been here."

He questioned them, "You guys didn't open the door for them?" "No, sir. Nobody's been here. Nobody came through the building." He said, "How did you get in?" I said, "I just opened up the door and I walked through the door." They never saw us because we were clothed in this garment.

INVISIBLE PROPHETS

"And he said unto him, Went not mine heart with thee, when the man turned again from his chariot to meet thee? Is it a time to receive money, and to receive garments, and olive yards, and vineyards, and sheep, and oxen, and menservants, and maidservants?"[27] This is scripture #2 of confirmation.

Naaman was head of the armies of Syria and a great friend of the king of Aram, who was concerned because Naaman was afflicted with leprosy. Naaman's wife had a handmaiden (a young Jewish girl who had been brought as a slave to Syria) who told Naaman's wife about Elisha the prophet. The king of Aram encouraged Naaman to seek for Elisha. So, the king of Aram sends a letter to the King of Israel requesting that he ask Elisha to heal Naaman. The king of Israel freaks out and rents his clothes for fear that Elisha will do something crazy and get him in trouble with Syria. Elisha hears what is going on and tells the king of Israel to send Naaman to him and he will find out that there is a prophet in Israel. I will abbreviate the story. Elisha sends Gehazi, his trusted servant, to Naaman and tells him to wash in the Jordan River seven times. After expressing a bit of disgust over the prophet's choice of the rivers, Naaman does what Elisha required. Naaman comes out of the water and he is healed.

We get to my point. When Gehazi goes to meet Naaman, he asks him for a bunch of money after the prophet of God had already told Naaman that he didn't have to give them anything. And Gehazi walks back into Elisha's house and Elisha says to the servant, "Where have you been?" Elisha already knew where Gehazi had been. Gehazi said, "I haven't been anywhere." Elisha replied, "Did not my spirit go with you?" Uh oh! Gehazi is exposed. The interesting point is that Elisha, from afar, saw everything that happened. He was one of the invisible prophets.

Went not my heart with thee? Elisha's words penetrate his servant's heart. I like how Barnes Notes interprets these words: "*Was I not with thee in spirit - did I not see the whole transaction, as if I had been present at it?*"[28] He uses the verb "went," because Gehazi has just denied his "going."

There is a similar situation with the Apostle Paul. There is a serious problem in the church in Corinth. There is a man who is having sexual immorality with his father's wife. Paul has made it clear that this act must be judged. The church is going through a difficult time, but they will do what is right. In a letter, they receive these words from Paul, words similar to Elisha. "*Although I am absent from you in body, I am present with you in spirit, and I have already pronounced judgment on the one who did this, just as if I were present.*"[29] Just as Elisha was there in spirit and saw the events, so did Paul watch over this assembly as the judgment took place. Scripture confirmation #3.

Was there something that he was clothed with that they couldn't see him? But he was actually there in the meeting. Elisha was actually with his servant. He actually walked with Gehazi and went with him. But Gehazi couldn't see him because Elisha was clothed in something that caused him to be invisible. It was the cloak.

One more Elisha story. *"Therefore the heart of the king of Syria was greatly troubled by this thing; and he called his servants and said to them, 'Will you not show me which of us is for the king of Israel?' And one of his servants said, 'None, my lord, O king; but Elisha, the prophet who is in Israel, tells the king of Israel the words that you speak in your bedroom.'*[30] Confirmation #4. We passed the number three. I have the confirmation I hoped for.

The king of Syria is furious. He cannot figure out how every move he makes and all of his information is revealed to the king of Israel. The king enquires of his occultic team, demanding that they tell him how this happens. Well, they don't know. They tell the king that "somehow Elisha is hanging out in your inner room and your inner court and he is hearing all your plans. With all the doors locked, he is still able to walk through the locked door, walk right into your chamber and hear your every conversation with the high officials." It is frustrating for the king, because Elisha is getting classified information and he is taking it back to the CIA of Israel, and he's telling them what the king was about to do.

I'm not talking about what will be seen on the earth, I'm talking about a higher mystical realm. Mystic just means *one that's close to God.* So, if you're wondering why I am saying *mystic,* it just means being close to the Lord.

In the 1900s, Rufus Jones, one of the well-known and well-loved Quakers, opened his heart for God's people to discover the power and passion of the mystics. Jones wrote these words concerning the mystic way.

"The Church, it is true, has never in any period quite sunk to the level of tradition and the automatism of habit, for it has always had beneath its system of organization and dogma a current, more or less hidden and subterranean, of vital, inward, spiritual religion, dependent for its power of conviction, not on books, councils, hierarchies or creeds,—not upon anything kept in cold storage,— but on the soul's experiences of eternal Realities."[31]

God will raise up people from the dust of the earth and bring them before kings. There will be those that have the mantle like Samuel, Ezekiel, Daniel, Isaiah, and the other prophets. There will be prophets over nations and God will give such accurate detailed information that governments will call upon these men to say, "What's really happening?"

THE FINGER OF DANIEL

Daniel operated in this kind of glory. I want to show you something you may have never seen before. *"In the same hour came forth fingers of a man's hand, and wrote over against the candlestick upon the plaster of the wall of the king's palace: and the king saw the part of the hand that wrote. Then the king's countenance was changed, and his thoughts troubled him, so that the joints of his loins were loosed, and his knees smote one against another."*[32]

Now most people have been taught that this was the *finger of God* that wrote on the wall. But the Lord told me this. "That was not the finger of the Lord. That was the finger of Daniel." And what happened was, he came into that place with the cloak of invincibility and invisibility and uncovered his hand so that the king could see his hand on the wall.

Only Daniel could be the one who translated what the wall said because he was the one who wrote on the wall. Before Daniel did the interpretation, the king said, *"that you shall be clothed with scarlet, and have a chain of gold about your neck, and shall be the third ruler in the kingdom."*[33] He walked in there and he said, "King, this is what the wall says." It says, "Your kingdom's coming to an end." The king was so impressed that he gave him a purple robe, a chain of gold, and a place of power in his kingdom. Daniel looks at the king and quickly responds, "Why do I need this robe? Your kingdom is coming to an end."

Daniel operated in the mystical prophetic realm that when he would get around people, they would have dreams. Daniel caused the king to have a dream. That's why he was able to go and interpret a dream when the king didn't even tell him what the dream was.

The king was a bit overwhelmed by the whole event. I am sure that the king thought that he had never seen this type of prophetic action before. The whole dialog between the king and his band of occultic seers was sort of funny. The king brought all those that operated in the occultic realm and asked them for the interpretation of the dream. I can hear one of them saying, "Okay, tell us your dream, and then we'll tell you what it means." The king says, "No, no. I've seen that before. You tell me what I dreamed and what is the interpretation." They look at each other and finally one of them says, "We can't do that."

You have the rest of the story. They bring Daniel in and he does what only Daniel can do.

There's a prophetic ministry that's coming and is available right now. This generation is going to step into the supernatural realm where even occultists won't be able to touch that dimension. They'll stand back and scratch their head and wonder where that level of prophetic ability came from. It is a high level of glory that is functioning and operating through a prophetic Daniel company that causes dreams and interprets them. This is the power of the Holy Spirit's anointing on God's servants.

DANIEL AND THE LIONS' DEN

There came a point when the other exalted leaders wanted to get rid of Daniel. They were jealous and afraid. His power and influence were growing. They came up with a plot. All the high powers under King Darius came up with this plan. They came before the king and said that they should give honor to the king by requiring that no person, for the time of 30 days, will ask a petition of their God. If they did, then they would be thrown into the lions' den. The king agreed. They knew this plot would work because Daniel would not go past a day without praying and petitioning his God. Well, it happened as they suspected.

Daniel knew the king had signed the decree. Daniel did not hide. He goes into his house, opens the windows, and starts praying, rather loudly. He prayed three times each day. He is caught. The king loves Daniel, but he signed the decree and they must keep it. So, Daniel is thrown into the den of lions. When you step into that place, you start to release what's on you and in you. It is the kingdom of God that is in you, including righteousness, peace, joy, and the Holy Ghost. The lions lose their appetite, get sleepy, and that is the end of that plot. It did not work. Oh, the life of a prophet of God!

God will take you to places that you don't even understand why you are there. You will be placed in unusual situations, all for the purposes of God. Your background, education, and where you come from, none of this matter. God will raise you up out of the dirt of the ground and set you among kings and princes to prophesy and to change political environments. The entirety of nations is hanging in the balance.

Many will be called to move in the glory of God and into dimensions they never dreamed of. God will use them to shift things that are going in the wrong direction. There is a generation, a kingdom generation, that is carrying a kingdom mandate by a company of people who are not trying to get taken out. God is calling us outside the church into places of incredible opportunity. God is doing a new thing on the earth. These *called ones* desire to bring the Kingdom down to earth. Suddenly, when the enemy is trying to bring turmoil to a nation and trying to bring upheaval, they will be able to step right in, and suddenly, overnight, something will shift and change for God's kingdom and glory. Will you join us?

3 / PANEGYRIS

A CELEBRATION OF THE SUPERNATURAL

"...to the general assembly and church of the firstborn who are registered in heaven, to God the Judge of all, to the spirits of just men made perfect..."[1]

GOD IS THE ONE I WASN'T LOOKING FOR! SUDDENLY, SUPERNATURALLY, unexpectedly, and out of nowhere, He shows up. I was not the chaser, for it was He who chased me. Serendipitously, I discovered what I was not looking for. All has changed. I have been given a new set of eyes. A bush becomes a mystery, a veil a revelation; angels appear, small shifts in my thinking as I am drawn toward the glorious assembly, the place of great joy.

Before diving into the depth of the *panegyris*, I want to create a biblical perspective for you. The word *panegyris* is a Greek word for a festive assembly. It is only used one time in the Bible and that is in Hebrews 12:23. The word *ecclesia* is often translated as assembly but is quite different from *panegyris*. "In the ekklesia there is the sense of an assembly coming together for the transaction of business, while the *panegyris* was a solemn assembly whose purpose was festal rejoicing."[2] At the mention of *panegyris*, one thinks of blissful singing, joyful dancing, and festive delight. *Panegyris* is a full expression of what life of the assembly is like in the presence of God, certainly an unending festive celebration.

Here is a final conclusion with the splendor of John Gill's words: "The *panegyris*, the holy assembly, met together, in the infinite mind of God, from all eternity; and in Christ, their head and representative, both then and in time; and at the last day, when they are all gathered in, they will meet together and what a joyful meeting it will be."[3]

The *panegyris* is the celebration of the supernatural in the gathering of His people. It is a celebration between the heavenly dimension and the earthly gathering. When God's people come together, there is delight that takes place and great joy fills the house. A holy and magnificent manifestation is pouring out from above, in the unseen realms.

Heaven's joyous company gradually materializes in our natural world. What occurs in heaven's assembly begins to manifest in the corporate gathering on the earth. Whatever God is saying is suddenly dispensed, and there's a celebration of the Spirit, a rejoicing amongst the saints as miracles, signs, and wonders begin to manifest, streaming like a river out of the heavenly dimension into our little domain.

That which is being released from above is being reflected on the earth. There is an inexplicable, unintended connectedness, a strange synchronicity that causes two realms to become as one. Whispered voices and hidden presences explode into joyous celebration of the saints in the unseen realm. It is the sound of the great cloud of witnesses of the just saints made perfect, gathered together with the saints in the earthly realm.

You are not by yourself. We are not alone. When we come into the realm of the spirit, something begins to happen. The unseen realm and earthly realm emerge as two realms in harmony and glorious celebration. Celebrate every encounter, sense it, inhale it, value it, and enjoy it for nothing lasts forever. When it's gone, you'll remember the feeling it gave you and that will probably leave you hungry for more.

FELLOWSHIP OF THE SAINTS

Most churches think of fellowship as a potluck dinner or a chat in the hallway before we go into the sanctuary or before we leave. The neighborhood bar is possibly the best counterfeit there is to real fellowship. It's an imitation, an escape from their painful reality. In that darkened place, you can share your failures and your secrets, and nobody will gossip, unlike most churches. Humans are hungry to be known and loved and will take a couple of beers as a counterfeit. Unfortunately, nothing ever changes.

The early church both blossomed and was greatly impacted by blessed fellowship. The fellowship they understood came from the Greek word, *koinonia,* which could be defined as a *sharing of a common life.* The beauty of life together, as conveyed in the early church, is the mutual loving assembly which they sought to maintain with one another. They lived in intimate friendship, sympathy, suffering, and persecution. They breathed the breath of endearing communion and cherished friendship with each other, mutually expressing their affection for each other.

When the power of the Holy Spirit fell upon the crowds in Jerusalem, thousands of diverse tribes were converted in one moment. This left the apostles with a difficult challenge. One of the problems was serving these groups who were separated from their family and friends. MacClaren's Exposition adds a very important cultural perspective of koinonia in Acts 2:24: "These three thousand, as was most natural, were cut off altogether from their ancient associations, finding themselves at once separated by a great gulf from their nation and its hopes and its religion, were driven together as sheep are when wolves are prowling around. And, being individually weak, they held onto one another, so that many weaknesses might make a strength, and glimmering embers raked together might break into a flame."[4]

Koinonia is unique in its fellowshipping in the realm of the Spirit. In 2 Corinthians 13:14, Paul blesses the church at Corinth with this Trinitarian Blessing: *The grace of the Lord Jesus Christ, and the love of*

God, and the communion of the Holy Ghost, be with you all. Amen. The grace of Jesus be with you. The love of God be with you. The communion of the Holy Spirit be with you. It is Paul's prayer that the believers become participants in fellowship with the Holy Spirit. May our spirits be joined in an amazing solidarity of the Holy Spirit.

CHURCH AND THE KINGDOM

The word for church is the Greek word *ekklesia*. *Ekklesia* means "called out," and generally implies an assembly and gathering of people. However, the original meaning of the word in ancient Greek meant a political assembly of citizens. I am of the conviction that *koinonia* will always come before *ekklesia*. Fellowship in the Spirit must take place before the *ekklesia* can actually meet together in perfect harmony. Now, ekklesia or church is not just coming and sitting in a pew. *Ekklesia* is a political term, which means the governmental gathering of God's saints to deliberate on kingdom affairs.

So, how do we put this together? God has called us to come together, not to just sit in a pew and participate in a church event. He has called us to be partakers of the kingdom. The word kingdom in the Greek is *basileia*, which is the royal rule or dominion or power.[5] And so it becomes necessary for the church in the 21st century to not just be participators, but to be partakers of the kingdom of God, to carefully consider all that is related to the government of heaven in the earth.

We have been called to bring a delegation that carries spiritual things to the earth in order to align earth to heaven. When we gather together, we are called to bring the royal rule and judgment of heaven to earth. Everything that does not look like heaven becomes our responsibility as a believer to see that thing shift. Jesus said, "*Thy kingdom come, thy will be done, on earth as it is in heaven.*"

There are two things I want to emphasize. First, the church is essentially supernatural, and to maintain the supernatural essence of the church, it is critical that each person fulfill their part. T. Austin-Sparks was a mentor to Watchman Nee and a most powerful influence on Leonard Ravenhill, David Ravenhill, and hundreds of others. Here is an excerpt from an article he wrote on the supernatural church:

> "First of all, Christianity and the Church (in truth, identical terms) came down from heaven, and have still unceasingly to be received and ENTERED from there. This is the very foundational truth of Christ Himself and of the Church in every individual incorporated into it. The teaching of the New Testament everywhere is this. The origin and home of Christ was in heaven. Everything originates from heaven. 'Bread from heaven' only means it is the sustaining, supporting power of heavenly resources <for the church>. It will be a SPIRITUAL magnet which will draw the Lord's people together in a SPIRITUAL fellowship."[6]

I understand that there are many that are disenchanted with the church and are tempted to give up, and there are those who have already abandoned the church. But your participation matters. You might feel burnt out, but we need to hear your voice. It is critical to gather God's people together and make one sound on the earth.

The second thing to consider is the role of the Church and the kingdom. There's something about the kingdom that God wants the Church to more fully understand. He wants us to understand that the kingdom is God's government on the earth and that we are ambassadors of the kingdom, reflecting God's will in these crucial times.

The opening proclamation of the New Testament is this: *The kingdom of the heavens has drawn near.*[7] There should be no conflict between Church and kingdom. We should be establishing the kingdom and building the Church. Witness Lee, a close associate of Watchman Nee, offers helpful thoughts on the relationship between the Church and the kingdom: "The Bible first presents the kingdom and thereafter presents the Church. Where the kingdom of the heavens is in authority, there a Church will be built up. A Church comes into being where a company of people accept the government of heaven. So, it would appear to be the presence of the kingdom that produces the Church. But the New Testament goes beyond that. That is only one half of the New Testament revelation; the other half is this —the Church brings in the kingdom. The Church that comes into being under the rule of heaven, by reason of her submission to the heavenly rule, deals with God's enemy."[8]

GATES, COVENANTS, AND ALTARS

The foundation of any kingdom is composed of three things: gates, covenants, and altars. Everything that is in your life is there because you allow it, not because God designed it, or that it came by chance. The things in your life are there because of the establishment of an altar, the cutting of covenant, and the opening of a gate.

In every area of your life, there is an altar that is either built to the natural realm or the supernatural realm. Let me say it this way: It is built to the flesh or is built to the Spirit. The Bible says, *"For he who sows to his flesh will of the flesh reap corruption, but he who sows to the Spirit will of the Spirit reap everlasting life."*[9] There are two fields, the field of the flesh and the field of the Spirit. The problem is not the seed. The problem is the field.

People believe that flesh is your natural body, but Paul isn't referring to your natural body. Paul is not talking about flesh and blood. He is talking about a realm that is dedicated to the fulfillment of selfish desires which is expressed in multiple ways. The seed cast into that field of the flesh becomes corrupted. In contrast, the seed sowed to the Spirit will reap life everlasting. Notice that one sows to *his* flesh and one sows to *the* Spirit. One spends his life indulging *himself* and the other spends their life serving *the* Spirit. An altar is built to the natural desires of the flesh and another altar is built to the supernatural life of the Spirit.

Anywhere there is an altar, you will find a sacrifice. Anywhere there is a sacrifice, a covenant is made. Psalm 50:5 establishes this truth: *"Gather My saints together to Me, Those who have made a covenant with Me by sacrifice."* Benson Commentary poetically wrote the first phrase with these words: "O ye angels, summon and fetch them to my tribunal." The saints are those in the *covenant,* and that covenant was ratified by *sacrifices.* As children of the covenant, they are the object of Jehovah's affection.

When you cut a covenant with God, it opens up the portal of heaven over your life so that the kingdom of God can come through your gate. I'm laying a foundation which you will see is important. Psalm 24:7 says, *"Lift up your heads, O ye gates; and be ye lifted up, ye everlasting doors; and the King of glory shall come in."* What you must understand is that gates do not have heads, nor do doors have the possibility to be everlasting. There is an everlasting covenant that God has cut with you. When David was receiving this revelation, actually what he was seeing was the new creation man, because there is a gate to the inside of us that will release the kingdom through us.

Gates in the natural are something that you enter through. The same is true in the spiritual. Every person has gates to their spirit, soul, and body. When you lift up your head and you open up your mouth, your mouth becomes a gate. Not only your mouth, but your eye is a gate, your ear is a gate. In fact, all five senses are gates into this natural realm. When you use them to glorify God, they will open that everlasting door so that the King of Glory can come in through the natural man.

IN ME, THROUGH ME

In his letter to the Church at Galatia, Paul deeply desired that they understand that it was *"God's pleasure to reveal His Son in me, that I might preach Him among the Gentiles."*[10] Paul was certain that he could not reveal Christ to the Galatians until a gate was opened and God revealed His Son in him. This is such an important revelation. There was no outward manifestation of Christ until Christ was revealed in him. An inward gate is opened. Christ was revealed *within* him. Then, the light of the knowledge of Christ lights up every corner of his soul. Another way to say it is that *the Christ within* is now released as *the Christ without.* There is a certain uniqueness of Christ being displayed through Paul.

Your body is a temple and it can release Him to the earth. That is exactly how the anointing operates. It comes *into you* and then *through you*. Paul triumphantly makes this declaration in Colossians 1:27, *"To whom God would make known what is the riches of the glory of this mystery among the Gentiles; which is Christ in you, the hope of glory."*

These words by Solomon and Paul appear to be a conundrum and a contradiction. First, let's look at Solomon's words in 1 Kings 8:27, *"Behold, the heaven and heaven of heavens cannot contain Thee; how much less this house that I have built?"* Then we turn to Paul's words in 1 Corinthians 3:16, *"Do you not know that you are the temple of God and that the Spirit of God dwells in you?"* The natural man does not understand spiritual realities. Only the spiritual man can. This means that your physical body transcends even the universe. As far out as technology can go, they can only see with the three-dimensional eye. But by the power of God, your spirit-filled body has access to all dimensions.

I don't believe that there is any coincidence that these particular verses were positioned at Psalms 24:7: *"Lift up your heads, O ye gates; and be ye lifted up, ye everlasting doors; and the King of glory shall come in."* Twenty-four hours a day, seven days a week, there's a prophetic decree that is constantly being proclaimed that God has made an everlasting covenant with His people. An open heaven is yours with full access. When you cut covenant with God, it gives you full access to receive and release that dimensional power into the earth.

A CITY AND A MOUNTAIN

The Church is the New Jerusalem, not to be confused with the Old Jerusalem. Galatians 4:26 gives us further perspective: *"But Jerusalem which is above is free, which is the mother of us all."* The New Jerusalem, the heavenly city, knows no bondage and is the mother of us all, nursed with the Spirit's impartation and nourished with heaven's revelation.

When we come together as the New Jerusalem coming down out of heaven and the body of Christ on earth, there is a connectivity that happens between the two dimensions. At all times, there are two worlds moving in congruent motion. Between the earthly and heavenly dimensions, moments exist when there is a strange synchronicity that transpires between these polar opposites, different dimensions drawn together by a divine magnetic force that, without planning or pushing, are drawn together into a divine unity of eternal purposes. In the middle of a holy epiphany, we fall into a sweet collaboration, when the heavenly realm is attracted and drawn toward the earthly realm. In times such as these, there is a delegation and a decree that comes into the council room of heaven that manifests in our world so that we know what the mind of God is in these critical moments.

When there is disunity in the body of Christ, the power and presence of God cannot demonstrate. But when we are in the Spirit, in unity, God commands the blessing because there's connectivity. *"Behold, how good and how pleasant it is for brethren to dwell together in unity! For there God commands the blessing."*[11] We recognize what's inside of me is something you need, and what's inside of you is something that I need. By the process of mutual contribution according to the gifts given, the body of Christ is enlarged, empowered, and embodied into one flesh. *"From whom the whole body fitly joined together and compacted by that which every joint supplieth, according to the effectual working in the measure of every part, maketh increase of the body unto the edifying of itself in love."*[12] I understand my place and gifting in the body of Christ. When I come to a congregation of the saints, I am there for a purpose. I come to represent and release what God has given to me. I usually minister in multiple ways according to the Spirit of God: revelation, impartation, prophetic words, healing, and more.

"And many nations shall come, and say, Come, and let us go up to the mountain of the LORD, and to the house of the God of Jacob; and he will teach us of his ways, and we will walk in his paths: for the law shall go forth of Zion, and the word of the LORD from Jerusalem."[13]

There will come a day when the prophetic message combined with supernatural power will draw the nations to the mountain of the Lord. That means that there's a revelation that we haven't known yet. The new revelation shall be so compelling and inspiring that all men shall hear and desire to become partakers of it. Many will be drawn to the mountain because they are hungry and long for more. Then, there will be those that do not go to God, because they know Him, but that they may know Him. They are drawn by a mighty impulse toward Him. They will seek revelation from those authorized and gifted by God to bring forth the revealed word of God.

ASSEMBLY OF THE SAINTS

"I will declare thy name unto my brethren: in the midst of the congregation will I praise thee."[14] The assembly of the saints is an exquisite picture of heavenly wonder. We gather together in the spirit of unity and are in the place of liberty, because where the spirit of the Lord is, there is liberty. *"Assembled together, with unveiled faces, we behold in a mirror the glory of the Lord being transformed into the same image as we go from glory to glory."*[15]

Do you comprehend the depth of Paul's words? This is not your typical gathering on a Sunday morning. Assembled now together, our faces not hidden, gazing in the mirror, shame is now gone, glory all around us, we are changed into His image, glory to glory, thank God we are home. Joined together in perfect union, the saints dance with joy to the songs of the King.

Hearing of the Word and seeing in the mirror, lives are changed. The reflected glory emanating from the face of Jesus comes into the assembly. The council of God is here to judge and declare.

"And the heavens will praise Your wonders, O LORD; Your faithfulness also in the assembly of the saints."[16] "Let them exalt Him also in the assembly of the people, And praise Him in the company of the elders."[17] "Praise the LORD! Sing to the LORD a new song, And His praise in the assembly of saints."[18]

We have the full council of God gathered together as one, heaven and earth, saints and elders, and heavenly hosts. I am not talking about the government we see in some churches. I am talking about godly and humble men and women who deeply care for all the concerns of the church.

The whole celestial company is gathered together to worship the wonders of God. The heavenly angels perfected in worship join with the assembly of the saints to declare the goodness and faithfulness of Jehovah. Wherever there is the unity of the brethren, there will always be a prophetic song. There will always be a message of the Spirit. Everything that is revealed during that particular gathering we will see a spiritual manifestation during the time of celebration. The message will carry a manifestation. Sometimes, the message doesn't necessarily come from behind the pulpit. Sometimes, it is through the collaboration of the assembly coming together and suddenly a realm of the Spirit begins to manifest. The spiritual demonstration is enveloped in a synchronicity and a synergy as the presence of God begins to be poured out upon us all.

HEAVENLY VOICES, GOLDEN VOLCANO

Years ago, I was in New Zealand. I was preaching on the presence of God and the *panegyris* of the spirit. At one point, the council room of heaven came. There was a celebration that hit the place, and feathers literally started to materialize all over the meeting room. Not only that, there were voices that started coming out of the speakers. People stopped listening to what I was saying. They were walking over to the speakers because there were angelic tongues and voices coming out of the speaker system.

At the same time, as I'm talking, suddenly I leave the meeting. I'm flying as fast as lightning through the air, and I come to a mountain in Auckland. It is interesting that Auckland has seven mountains. They are actually volcanoes. But the locals call them mountains. My body is in the meeting, but my spirit is gone and in a volcano in Auckland. Try to figure that out theologically. Paul said, "Whether in the body or out of the body, I do not know, but God knows." It must have been something like Paul's experience.

I'm flying at this mountain and eventually enter it. Below me, I see all this gold and silver. Overwhelmed by the sight, I cry out, "My God, there's millions of dollars down here." I'm in this volcano and looking down and I'm seeing all this gold and silver and stuff. At one point, I come back into the meeting and I speak out, "There's gold and silver in the mountains of the city that is worth millions of dollars." I speak as though it is a prophetic sign, "Tonight, people are going to get gold crowns in their mouth." There was such a unified front amongst us as we experienced the realm of the spirit in our midst. During that meeting, people did get gold crowns in their mouth. Three weeks after I left, scientists discovered that underneath the mountains in Auckland, there were loads of gold worth multiplie millions of dollars. What you have to realize is that it's debatable whether that gold was actually ever there before.

I honestly believe that it was something God showed me in the heavenly realm that I was meant to decree and declare over that nation. It didn't exist until there was a delegation and a spoken word that was released through a corporate body. The moment that I said it, it was like an atomic bomb hit that meeting and people started screaming. What heaven was celebrating, those that were on the earth felt it in their spirit because your spirit will always testify to spiritual things. Your spirit will leap on the inside of you when you understand what is being spoken belongs to you, for it is your portion.

THE CLOUD OF WITNESSES

Before moving to Hebrews 12, it would be important to summarize Hebrews 11, which has a great lineup of heroes in the Hall of Fame that are part of the cloud of witnesses. Hebrews 11 renders a splendid portrait of the men and women who triumphed by faith, even though many of them suffered at the hands of their persecutors. This company of biblical legends believed God and pursued His promises to the end of their lives. We will need this verse before moving into chapter 12: "*God having provided something better for us that they should not be made perfect without us.*"[19]

This segues into chapter 12, verse 1 and 2: "*Wherefore seeing we also are compassed about with so great a cloud of witnesses, let us lay aside every weight, and the sin which doth so easily beset us, and let us run with patience the race that is set before us, Looking unto Jesus the author and finisher of our faith; who for the joy that was set before him endured the Cross, despising the shame, and is set down at the right hand of the throne of God.*"

Let's take one step back into the Old Testament, a verse that will add biblical perspective. "*Moreover, brethren, I would not that ye should be ignorant, how that all our fathers were under the cloud, and all passed through the sea...*"[20] The Israelites were encompassed with the pillar of cloud in the desert, and with the clouds of glory on Mount Sinai. The covering cloud of the Old Testament was "a symbol of the divine presence with the Israelites, as it was on Mount Sinai, and in the tabernacle and temple; was a protection of them, being in the daytime as a pillar of cloud to screen them from the scorching heat of the sun, and in the night time as a pillar of fire to preserve them from beasts of prey, as well as in both to guide and direct them in the way; and the cloud was a type of Christ, who is our cover."[21]

When you consider the depth of these words written by the author of Hebrews you must agree that this is really powerful. Hebrews 11 gives us what we need to determine that the cloud of witnesses at least included those mentioned in Hebrews 11. The angelic host once bore witness to the patriarchs, prophets, kings, and host of men and women who testified to their faith. Although the word for *marturon* reflects martyrdom, it does have a broader sense in our common use of the word witness. Clement of Alexandria added his own view of a cloud of witnesses: "We have so great a cloud, a numberless multitude above us, like a cloud, 'holy and translucent.'"[22]

"*For this cause I bow my knees unto the Father of our Lord Jesus Christ, Of whom the whole family in heaven and earth is named.*"[23] Though it might seem that the saints in heaven and the saints on earth might be two families, it is not the case. We are one family under God. Paul recognizes all families, in heaven or on earth, as one, and the whole family finds their name associated with the Father.

This is Spurgeon's perspective on this matter: "The inhabitants of heaven and believers on earth might seem to be two orders of beings, yet in truth they are *one family*. To this thought I call your attention, hoping that you may enter into that *one communion*, in which saints above are bound up with saints below in the indissoluble kinship in Christ which holds us as much as ever in one sacred unity."[24]

What God is doing in the heavens, He also wants to manifest on the earth. But His body in the heavens must have a body on the earth that will co-labor together to accomplish the Father's will.

Some of the church is finally understanding that the spirit world is more *real* than we are. Let me illustrate my point. It was in about 2014 and my wife Brynn and I were in the city of Beijing, China. Question for you. Have you ever spoken in Chinese tongues? It's awesome.

I was in a meeting, and the realm of heaven came down. It's a very unique realm. There is a realm of the anointing and glory. It is a mystical realm, like the *panegyris* realm that when you cross over as you enter into celebration and festivity. So, we are in this meeting and the power of God is hitting people all over the room. As we are praying, people are going down. This one young man who never experienced a vision, well, he went into a vision and saw an angelic lion. It was amazing what was happening.

There is mystical chaos everywhere. I am watching what is happening at the back of the room. I'm standing in the front just looking, while at the same time, there is a mist drifting into the room. At the back, a man walks into the room. He looked like he had been on the earth for awhile. It was more like he left the earth and came back.

While he's standing in the back, this Chinese man is staring at me. I'm seeing this with my eyes and I'm thinking, "What in the world?" Without a doubt, I was sure that he had just come right out of the cloud and was just standing in the back. I don't know who he was. To this day, I don't know who he was. He had come out of the cloud of witnesses, stood in the back of the room, nodded his head at me, and walked right through the back of the church again.

PASSING THROUGH THE HEAVENS

"Seeing then that we have a great High Priest who has passed through the heavens, Jesus the Son of God, let us hold fast our confession."[25]

"He who descended is Himself also He who ascended far above all the heavens, so that He might fill all things."[26]

As the high priest passed through the holy place to enter into the Most Holy Place, so Jesus ascended through the heavens to take His place on the throne. The prophet Isaiah cried out in Isaiah 64:1, *"Oh that You would rend the heavens and come down." The heavens have been torn and the heavens are open, forever.*

The heavens have been opened and will never close again. Standing before an open heaven, the altar has been built, the covenant made, and the gates have been opened. When we begin to decree and declare, none of our words fall to the ground. The sound of our voice creates an echo that ascends into the heavens and a counter echo sends them back down to the earth. When heaven responds, a manifestation will take place because you are not speaking your own words.

Peter makes a clear directive to those who will speak to God's people: *"If anyone speaks, let him speak as the oracles of God."* An oracle is a vessel that speaks forth the counsel of God and decrees and declares the Word of Jesus. His words come from God, and are breathed and spoken by Him, containing His mind and will, and are authoritative and infallible.

GOD SPEAKS

Several years ago, I was sitting with Paul Keith Davis. My wife Brynn and I were having breakfast with him. Paul Keith has a great collection of the works of William Branham. We were sitting at breakfast and eating when he said to me, "I want you to hear something." So, he pulls out a recording of Branham and he says, "I want you to listen to this very carefully." I was listening to it and Branham is seeing an open-eyed vision of the demonic realm. He's seeing Satan challenging with sickness and disease over the people and he commands sickness and disease to leave the people. And he says, "Satan, I decree and declare." And he is challenging Satan in this meeting.

Suddenly, on the audio system, you hear a wind blow into the meeting, and you hear a voice in the wind, and it is not over the microphone. It comes through the speakers, but it's not Branham's voice. It's God's voice audibly captured on the recording and the voice says, "Amen."

And then it says, "I Am God. Amen." Branham speaks to the congregation, "Did you hear that? Did you hear that? That's almighty God testifying to His Word." Then you hear the people screaming all over the entire meeting as they were getting healed. What was decreed in the heavenlies was being released into the earth, and the testimony of God's voice came into the midst of the congregation because of a spirit of unity.

MOUNT ZION AND PRAYING IN THE SPIRIT

"But you have come to Mount Zion and the city of the living God, the heavenly Jerusalem. To the innumerable company of angels, to the general assembly and the church of the firstborn who are registered in heaven. To the God, the judge of all, to the spirits of just men made perfect, to Jesus the mediator of the new covenant, and to the blood that speaks, that sprinkling that speaks better things than that of Abel."[27]

When did we come to Mount Zion? We came as a citizen when we were born again. But when do we go and access Mount Zion? Whenever we are in the Spirit. When we are in the Spirit, we are able to go up the mountain, because in our own strength we can't do it. While you have been getting citizenship in the heavenly realm, you have to be *in the Spirit* in order to access that heavenly dimension.

Jude 1:20 says, *"Praying in the Spirit."* I believe that what Jude is actually talking about is actually praying in the spiritual realm. Here is the awesome part. When you pray in the Spirit, that is, in the environment of His influence, your prayers become effective. Praying in the Spirit, in the spiritual realm, is a dimension of prayer that is amazing. When we add this point, it becomes even more astounding. *"And I will pray to the Father, and he shall give you another Comforter, that he may abide with you forever."*[28] The Greek word for Comforter is *parakletos* and it means comforter and counselor. But the literal meaning is *called to the side of another.* Jesus sent His Holy Spirit to be your alongside one, your counselor, and your teacher. When you are praying in the spiritual realm, you are not alone. The teacher and the comforter are with you, leading and directing you.

A LION GOES TO CHURCH

Several years ago, there was a moment when I was conducting meetings in Durban, South Africa. A friend of mine has an amazing church in Durban and I was excited to be there. I'm there on a Sunday morning and I have started ministering. Abruptly, I go into a trance. I am standing there and suddenly this lion walks into the room. I go, "What the?" I followed up with this response, "I'm in Africa. I mean, a lion is walking through the meeting right now." The lion walks up to me and starts talking to me. What is one expected to do? So, I talked back in what I was sure was English. I'm in the Spirit and I'm having a conversation with a lion that's in the room. I start the conversation with these words, "What are you doing here, lion?" The lion says to me, "My name is Cyrus and I'm a breaker angel and I've come to roar over people."

Abruptly, I snap out of it and this lady on the third row says, "Excuse me, sir. Excuse me!" I said, "Yes." She said, "You were just speaking in my language." I said, "What was that? English?" She said, "No. Did you not hear yourself?" I said, "Well, yeah. I was speaking English." She said, "You weren't speaking English. You were speaking Zulu."

I responded, "What did I say?" She said, "Well, you said that the lion of the tribe of Judah is King forever." The power of God hit that place. It was off the charts, because what is in the Spirit wants to materialize in the natural.

HARVEST

"Here is the patience of the saints: here are those who keep the commandments of God and the faith of Jesus. Then I heard a voice from heaven saying to me, 'Write, blessed are the dead who die in the Lord from now on. Yes,' says the spirit, 'That they may rest from their labors and their works follow them.'"[29]

When I'm talking about the cloud of witnesses, I am not talking about necromancy, because necromancy is where dead spirits speak through an individual. What I am talking about is what Jesus said about Abraham, that Abraham is alive. *"Truly, truly, I say to you, if anyone keeps my word, he will never see death. Your father Abraham rejoiced that he was to see my day; he saw it and was glad."*[30]

Everyone that's in heaven is alive. That being true then, according to the Scriptures, the cloud of witnesses can speak to you, but never through you! Don't you remember that you are surrounded with a great cloud of witnesses, a company of God's people who have finished their race? They have kept the commandments of God and the faith of Jesus.

Those that have passed on are resting from their labors because they are in the cloud of witnesses. However, their works are constantly, continuously speaking on the earth and their mantles are actually in the earth because a mantle never goes to heaven. It always gets dropped. That's what Elisha was hoping for. And if you pick up that mantle, you can enter into the works of the Father and reap the harvest.

"And I looked, and behold a white cloud, and upon the cloud one sat like unto the Son of man, having on his head a golden crown, and in his hand a sharp sickle. And another angel came out of the temple, crying with a loud voice to him that sat on the cloud, Thrust in thy sickle, and reap: for the time is come for thee to reap; for the harvest of the earth is ripe. And he that sat on the cloud thrust in his sickle on the earth; and the earth was reaped."[31]

I believe that in every generation, there is a harvest, and the cloud of witnesses and those that have labored before us are watching to see what we are going to do because their ceiling has now become our floor. They are waiting and watching with expectation for us to finish out the prophetic scroll that was released into the earth through prophecy, through declaration, through gatherings of the saints.

We will enter into those same labors and we will begin to work alongside them, and we will begin to manifest the same works that they did. When the glory comes, the cloud appears, and on that cloud is Jesus with a crown of gold and a sharp sickle. We are all as one, the heavenly host, those in the earthly realm, and Christ dwells in our midst. Thrust in the sickle and reap the harvest, for the earth is ready.

We are about to step into something that is ripe and ready. I believe that we are in a time of activation and impartation. Those in the heavenly dimensions will open the way for a new generation to enjoy the harvest.

THE 4 ORDERS OF SUPERNATURAL TRAVEL

"Giving thanks to the Father who has qualified us to be partakers of the inheritance of the saints in the light. He has delivered us from the power of darkness and conveyed us into the kingdom of the Son of His love."[1]

IN NATURE, THERE IS AN INVISIBLE LINE, VERY REAL AND DEFINITE, ABOVE which you will never find a snake. Early settlers in America referred to this line as "the snake line." There is a level of living that is higher and more desirable than a mediocre spiritual life that is below what was meant for you. In Christ, we have been elevated above the line. Paul addressed the issue of life above the line with these words:

"If ye then be risen with Christ, seek those things which are above, where Christ sitteth on the right hand of God."[2]

You should not settle for an inferior and insignificant life, when there are greater possibilities for you. It is at this point in the book where I want to elevate your experiences in the supernatural and enlighten the part of your life you don't see or know. I want to get you above the earthly line.

CHANGE OF STATE

Colossians 1:12-13 is the foundation for the things that I will deliver to you in this chapter: *"Giving thanks to the Father who has qualified us to be partakers of the inheritance of the saints in the light. He has delivered us from the power of darkness and conveyed us into the kingdom of the Son of His love..."*

There are six key elements in these two verses that are part of a progression that will direct us to the major concepts that will be addressed in this chapter.

Giving thanks to the Father: As you begin to mature in your experiences and knowledge of the supernatural, there is a danger that could negatively affect you, the emergence of pride and ingratitude. While you remain humble in all you do and thankful to Father for the gifts and anointing which He has given you, then you will continue to advance in all that Father desires for you. Humility, not hubris! Thankfulness, not thanklessness.

qualified us: The qualification is not based upon your merit, but because of God's favor. There is nothing we have earned. Grace is the qualifier for all that we are called to do.

to be partakers of the inheritance of: Moffat's translation reads 'to share the lot.' The participation in the inheritance is given to every believer, without striving for it. It appears that the issue of inheritance was on the Apostle Paul's mind a lot, especially in the Ephesians letter. Paul sums up the inheritance with his words in Ephesians 1:3, *"Blessed be the God and Father of our Lord Jesus Christ, who hath blessed us with <u>all spiritual blessings in heavenly places</u> in Christ..."*

the saints in the light: "Light begins in the believer descending from 'the Father of lights' by Jesus, 'the true light,' and is perfected in the kingdom of light, which includes knowledge, purity, love, and joy."[3] An unknown author said that light is the element and atmosphere of God. Others associate light with sight and glory. Certainly, in this passage, it is the light of the kingdom of God. Light rules by its enlightenment. When the light of life shines and rules, it is a kingdom. *"Again Jesus spoke to them, saying, 'I am the light of the world. Whoever follows me will not walk in darkness, but will have the light of life.'"*[4]

He has delivered us from the power of darkness: Jesus has set us free from darkness, having rescued us from that state of ignorance and error, of impenitence and unbelief, and has brought us to a place where we now know the truth, and the truth makes us free from the guilt and power of sin. Strong's Concordance adds this insight: "methistemi from meta = denoting change of place or condition + histemi =place, stand and literally means to remove or transfer from one place to another."[5]

conveyed us into the kingdom: The Greek word for convey is *mathesstama*. One perspective of its meaning is that while still in the body, we have been taken out of darkness and moved (translated, transferred, conveyed) into a place of light. Ellicott's Commentary presents it this way: "a word properly applied to the transplanting of races, and the settlement of them in a new home."[6] Barclay's Commentary has this to offer: "This is a word with a special use. In the ancient world, when one empire won a victory over another, it was the custom to take the population of the defeated country and transfer it."[7] Translation is the key to this chapter.

LIVING IN THE LIGHT

"If we live in the Spirit, let us also walk in the Spirit."[8] In this letter to the Galatians, Paul seeks to enable them to understand that if we live in the Spirit, we will have the availability to actually walk in light. The life and light which the Spirit quickens needs human participation. It is not an occasional visit, but an abiding presence of the Spirit with us, within us. Jesus spoke these words and added to the power of the light: *"I am the light of the world. Whoever follows me will never walk in darkness, but will have the light of life."*[9] The impression of the words of Jesus are clear: those who follow Christ have a light that will guide them in these difficult times, but, through participation in the life of the Messiah, they will actually possess that light in themselves.

Since God has translated us from a kingdom of darkness into a kingdom of light, we now have the availability to enter into the realm of the Spirit. Since we do not walk in the darkness, but in the light, then we can walk in the unseen realms and enjoy the riches of the kingdom of God.

These are realms that are unseen by the naked eye. We can't see them with our regular eyes, our three-dimensional eye. But there's a realm that we can enter into that is a higher place, a place of the glory of God. Back to Paul's words on translation, the *mathesstama* signifies that we have been relocated, transferred from darkness to light. By the power of God's kingdom, we have been transformed and translated and can now walk in the unseen realms of God's glory.

"The word is a lamp unto my feet, and a light unto my path."[10] The Word is a lamp, a candle, a torch, and a light for direction and insight. It is important to understand that the Word of God is not just what is written on the page. God's Word comes to us in a variety of ways. Read the Words of Jesus: *"And Jesus answered him, saying, It is written, That man shall not live by bread alone, but by **every word of God**."*[11] The important issue is that the Word, in whatever way it comes, is a living source. Light is a source which every believer can tap into. The light of life is supernatural energy and force. Walking in the light is walking in the glory, for the glory of the Lord is the light of God. Paul wrote these words concerning light and the glory: *"For God, who commanded the light to shine out of darkness, hath shined in our hearts, to give the light of the knowledge of the glory of God in the face of Jesus Christ."*

Moving on. You can see that I am pushing forward to establish a foundation with all these verses. The prophet Isaiah offers this interesting perspective: *"Who are these who fly like clouds, like the doves to their windows?"*[12] In multitudes so numerous, they appear as a dense cloud, a cloud of witnesses. They are a company of glory carriers, a community of glory believers that will walk in the unseen realm. They will rise to a place of revelation, a place of living in the light of life. They will receive impartation fanned by the Spirit God. They will walk in the Spirit, not the flesh. A nation flying like clouds, hungry and they will be fed, empty wells will be filled, broken hearts will be healed, and prodigals will be translated to home.

TRANSLATING BY FAITH

I have laid the foundation and now it is time for unveiling the Four Orders of Supernatural Travel. First, I want to establish this critical point that is set in 1 Corinthians 13:2: *"And though I have the gift of prophecy, and understand all mysteries, and all knowledge; and though I have all faith that I should remove mountains, if I have not charity, I am nothing."* This word "remove" is the word *mathesstama*,[13] that I have already mentioned, and we will be building on that word.

However, this is my critical point before moving on. The *love* principle is the essential requirement for those that want to move mountains, walk in the supernatural realms, experience angels, and experience translations, trans-relocations, and transfigurations. Love is what it is all about.

There has to be a reason why the power of God is at work. God doesn't want us to just translate in the Spirit just for the experience. If you've ever known or studied someone that's had a supernatural translation or teleportation or that has gone somewhere in the Spirit, there was always a reason behind that particular manifestation. In most cases, it was to help someone or to save somebody. This needs to be our motivation when we are moving into this realm. *Love is everything.*

Translation is the very first order of supernatural travel. What do I mean by translation? Translation is the process of moving something or someone to another place, from earth to heaven, or from that place or that person to another place or person. In this case, it is only by the spirit, not the physical body. It is just your spirit that is traveling. Do not miss that point.

By translation, you can move things through the Spirit from one place to another. You can take something in the Spirit, or in prayer, and move it to the throne of God for consultation or prayer.

"And I know such a man—whether in the body or out of the body I do

not know, God knows—how he was caught up into Paradise and heard inexpressible words, which it is not lawful for a man to utter."[14] It took Paul 14 years before he shared his experience. Evidently, the time was right for him to reveal the visions and revelations he received from the Lord.

In verses two and three, his letter seems to indicate he is sharing an experience of someone else. However, it is the consistent position of the theologians that it was Paul sharing his story. In verse 7, he gives it away when he writes in his first narrative speech, *"in order to keep me from becoming conceited."*

For the purpose of my teaching, let's consider the perspective of German theologian Heinrich Dissen on Paul's catching away: "In that ecstasy his lower consciousness had so utterly fallen into abeyance, that he could not tell afterwards whether this had fallen place by means of a temporary withdrawal of his spirit, or whether his whole person, the body included had been snatched away."[15] I believe that in this case, Paul's spirit was translated to the third heaven. Either way, it is clear that theologians believe that both are possible.

When you are in a time of intense prayer, your spirit will take you into the heavenly realm. Sometimes, there are things that you can't see in the natural world, but they are things that you're dealing with. For instance, when you go into the Spirit and you begin to pray, there may be a burden on you about something, and it's not even a tangible object, but yet, by the spirit of translation, you are able to bring that into the spirit realm, into heavenly places. You can take something into heaven like situations, circumstances, different things that can be translated into heavenly realms for the purpose of prayer and conversation.

That means you can take your children into heaven, even if they don't believe. Even if they are unbelievers and they are not saved, you can take them in the spirit to the throne and present them before God in prayer and petition. This same principle would apply for any need or concern you have, and you can take them to the heavenly places. You could move a financial need into that place, or your children, your husband, your wife, or your business. Whatever you see that is a need, bring it out of the darkness and expose it to the light of the supernatural place.

If you feel these challenging situations have created an atmosphere of darkness, then you can transform them by translating them into the kingdom of light. By the power of the Spirit, you can translate these concerns out of darkness and bring them into light.

This is just the first realm of teaching on spiritual travel. I am teaching you a very deep principle on how to see results when you pray in the Spirit and are released, or *translated*, into heavenly realms. When darkness is defying circumstances, you can bring the light over that and create dramatic change. There is no circumstance that you could not apply to translation in the Spirit.

This is the process of going into another dimension outside the earthly realm. You are now in heavenly places and ready to bring changes to the earth. Whatever troubles you can be presented to the light in the heavenly places. The more that you walk in the light of the Word, the more that darkness has to flee.

The best Scripture that I can give you for translation is found in Ezekiel 8:3: "*He stretched out the form of a hand, and took me by a lock of my hair; and the Spirit lifted me up between earth and heaven, and brought me in visions of God to Jerusalem.*" What looked like a hand, stretches out toward Ezekiel and grabs him by the lock of his hair. The touch of the hand is followed by the action of the Spirit. Matthew Henry says that he was conveyed in spirit to Jerusalem.

There were many in the Scriptures that moved in the Spirit like Ezekiel, but not in their physical body. They were translated into another place by the Spirit. Their physical body stayed on earth, but their spirit went to other dimensions. This is called *translation* and this is the first form of spiritual travel we are talking about.

Let me share how God opened the supernatural realm to me. I was in a meeting years ago, when I was in my early 20s. I was in this meeting and I was taken in the Spirit, away from the earth, and I was brought to heaven. This is one of the very first times that I ever went into heaven. In this encounter, I approached these two very large double doors. I was walking up these stairs. It was so surreal, so incredible. Suddenly, the doors came open and there was a young boy standing there. It seemed to me that he was about five years old. It was the weirdest thing... he looked just like *me*.

I stared into his eyes. I could not stop looking. I was so shocked when I saw this young person. At that point, I immediately fell. It felt like I fell out of heaven and back into the meeting. I had no idea what had happened.

For years, I speculated about this event and could not figure out the meaning of the heavenly encounter. When I got married to my wife Brynn, I had an encounter, and the Lord spoke to me. When we found out that she was pregnant and we were going to have a son, it all became real. Now I understood the boy in heaven. The Lord wanted to show me my son, who is now going to be turning 12. The Lord spoke to me and said, "The boy that you saw in that encounter was your son and you must name him Nehemiah." Over the years, many people have wondered why I named him Nehemiah. Here is the reason. There was a man that I knew from the Dominican Republic of Congo that I had met there, and he deeply impacted my life during my time there. The Lord told me to name my son after that man. The person that I had seen in the heavenly encounter before I was married was my son. It was an incredible, surreal moment. We didn't even know the gender of the baby at the time. Without knowing, I told my wife Brynn, "We were going to have a son, his name is Nehemiah, and I've already met him in heaven."

When he became about five years old, I was sitting there and he ran into the room, and it was like such a surreal moment because the face that I had seen in heaven was standing right before me. It was a powerful moment, but you must understand that the realm of translation is very real, and God wants to bring us into this realm. He wants to bring us into these heavenly dimensions.

DEALING WITH WITCHCRAFT

Moving into a person's dream can be dangerous. If you were sent to someone's dream by the Lord and you're not trying to make it happen, then you can give them an impartation and offer some wisdom as you traveled in the spirit, by the will of the Lord. You never do any of this by your own abilities. You do this by faith in Jesus Christ and by His will. If you are doing this by your will, then you are doing this illegally, which is an act of witchcraft.

You are moving into occultism when you go into someone else's dream life and you have not been invited. Those involved in witchcraft can bring darkness into your dreams. They'll attack you in the night.

Some of you probably had an encounter when there was something dark that was in your dream. You met someone in your dream, and you knew they were wicked. This is when people move into your dreams, but by witchcraft.

There's a difference between translation and astral projection. Now, what is the difference between translation and astral projection? The difference is that every person that has been born again, according to John chapter 3, no longer has a silver cord, which you can find in Ecclesiastes 12:6: *"Or ever the silver cord be loosed, or the golden bowl be broken, or the pitcher be broken at the fountain, or the wheel broken at the cistern."* Some theologians believe that this verse translates, from Hebrew, to be the spinal cord and indicates various ways a man can die (references to the silver cord, the golden bowl of the pitcher).

Psychics and those involved in witchcraft believe that the silver cord connects you to your physical body. It can help you navigate around the area near your physical body and it helps you to return to your physical reality whenever you want.

Those who embrace the dark side of the silver cord are not a part of the light of God. Impartation and translation are quite different from astral projection. Your inheritance as a born-again believer is to move in the Spirit. Satanists, witches, warlocks, occultists, and people that have not been born of the Spirit are moving there illegally. They're coming in through a spirit guide, a familiar spirit, or something that you've opened yourself up to that has allowed them to come in.

If you have hidden sins in your life, then it will open that dark realm. If so, you need to make sure that you apply the blood of Jesus. With those that are born again, they no longer have a silver cord because they've been born from above. They are a new creation in Christ Jesus. These individuals are not coming to destroy you, but to bring impartation to you.

This is the way that you will see this activated, through dreams, in a biblical way. Translation primarily happens with dreams, which is the first level. Remember, it is God who will send you there. You never send yourself. If you are sending yourself, it is witchcraft. If God is sending you there, it's for an impartation. When you recognize that, there's a purpose behind it.

Although these impartations primarily happen in dreams, there can be occasions where they happen while you are in prayer. The majority of time that you experience the realm of translation, it will be when you go in your dreams. Why is that? It is because you're going to be in a place of reception and your brain is not going to be trying to block your spirit and your soul from focusing on the spirit. Don't let the mind get in your way.

HEAVEN IS REAL

While teaching on transportation, it is important to remind you that heaven is a real place. It's as real as the earth is real. If you were taken there, you have been to a real place. Just because you can't see something with your naked eye doesn't mean that it doesn't exist. It's just on a higher plane of reality and revelation. In Philippians 3:20, Paul wrote these words: *"For our conversation is in heaven; from whence also we look for the Saviour, the Lord Jesus Christ."*

The original expression rendered *conversation* is a word of very extensive meaning, [16]implying that our citizenship, our thoughts, and our affections are already in heaven. The Ethiopic version renders it, "we have our city in heaven." Someone said that our mind is on earth, but our country is in heaven. There are two great communities in the universe, earth and heaven. There are laws and institutions in both realms. It is obvious that heaven is real!

The earth has a domain which is three-dimensional. That's where you live in the conscious realm. But as you go into heaven, you're leaving this conscious three-dimensional state and entering into a higher reality or sphere of existence. Heaven is just as real as this world. It's just unseen.

When you are moving from our world, you are moving from *consciousness* into a *subconscious realm*, or you can move into a subconscious realm where you fall asleep and are at rest. Paul described his experience with these words: "I don't know if I was in the body or out of the body."

How do I get myself into a place where I'm traveling at night? I have had this experience many times. I am traveling in the spirit to various locations, whether I'm going to Africa, or I'm going over to minister in the Middle East, because there's somebody that's there that I need to minister to.

I'm moving by dreams or I'm moving into heaven during the night, and I know that I'm doing it. See, that is the key. A lot of you have done it, but you aren't aware of it. The question that you are probably asking is, "How do I do it?" There are three keys to translating in the spirit.

KEYS TO TRANSLATING IN THE SPIRIT NUMBER ONE: PRAYING IN TONGUES

Praying in tongues will open your spirit. Tongues is the spiritual language of heaven that opens your spirit so that you can enter into the realm of the spirit. The language of the Spirit will take you into the spirit.

Every night, before I go to sleep, I pray in tongues. I pray in tongues until I fall asleep. I am conscious, totally aware of myself, as I pray in the Spirit. I consciously pray in tongues until I begin to fall into the realm of the Spirit.

While you're praying in tongues, your whole body begins to feel your spirit. Your physical body is on the earth, but the process of speaking in tongues activates your spirit so that it can begin to travel where God wants to take you.

How do I pray? I pray in this way: "Lord, tonight use me while I'm asleep. I want You to take me in the Spirit." Then, I begin to pray in tongues and start to fall into that realm where my brain is no longer working; in other words, I have tuned into another source.

THE MIND OF THE MAKER

If I ask you to touch your mind, what will you do? Most of you will touch your brain. That's because we don't know what to do with brain/mind issues. Let's ask a professional what the difference is between the brain and the mind. "No doubt the brain plays an incredibly important role. But our minds cannot be confined to what's inside our skull, or even our body, according to a definition first put forward by Dan Siegel, a professor of psychiatry at UCLA School of Medicine. A meeting of 40 scientists across disciplines, including neuroscientists, physicists, sociologists, and anthropologists. This is what they came up with. It is a key component of the mind: the emergent self-organizing process, both embodied and relational, that regulates energy and information flow within and among us."[17]

Your brain is a muscle in your head. Your brain is a biochemical organ. Your mind is connected to your spirit and your soul. Both the soul and the mind are connected to the Creator and the heavenly realms.

All thought originates from this place of the mind, but where is it getting its source from? The spirit. All your ideas come from this place. No person has an original thought. Your mind is connected to your spirit and flows into your soul. Everything comes from the spirit.

When you understand that, then you'll understand that when you are praying in tongues, you're bypassing your brain and you're beginning to move into the mind of Christ. When you're praying in the language of the Spirit, you're moving into Christ's consciousness.

When you're doing that, then that's when your imagination can be changed, your mind can be changed. It can all be rearranged.

That's why Paul said to renew the spirit, namely the *spirit* of your mind. "*And be not conformed to this world: but be you transformed by the renewing of your mind, that you may prove what is that good, and acceptable, and perfect, will of God.*"[18] It is the will of God that we go through a transformation in view of that higher form of existence. How do you get there? By the transformation of your mind! It is the regenerating power of the Holy Spirit that leads to a rectification of the mind.

Let's reiterate. Speaking in tongues is primarily how we activate translation in the Spirit. While praying in tongues, we are opening up our spirit to lord it over our soul. Your mind is a functioning part of the soul and is for this reason that the mind must be renewed by the Holy Spirit.

We want our spirit to have domination over our mind, so we can think the thoughts of heaven. We begin to think like God. We want to have *Christ-consciousness*. As this transformation of the mind increases, we begin to think according to the mind of Christ. Our eyes are now opened so we can see the unseen world, the way God sees it.

KEYS TO TRANSLATING IN THE SPIRIT NUMBER TWO: THE WORD OF GOD

The second thing I focus on is to get to a place where my soul is subject to my spirit, and that is meditating on the Word of God. The Word of God opens me up. Why? Because if I can find it in the Word, then I have a platform that I can springboard off of. I find comfort in being backed up by the Word.

God wants our thoughts to be His thoughts so that our actions will be in line with His actions. John's words are so encouraging and enticing. Consider them: "*If you abide in me, and my words abide in you, ask whatever you wish, and it will be done for you.*"[19]

Whatsoever you ask shall be done for you! That sounds scary. Before you can ask at that level, you must be living in the Word and the Word living in you. "The believer in Christ, full of his words, ever-more consciously realizing union with Christ, charged with the thoughts, burning with the purposes, filled with words of Jesus, will have no will that is not in harmony with the Divine will."[20] There is a price to be paid before you can be translating at that level. Meditate on the Word and your soul will be controlled and your spirit set free to fly like an eagle. Charles Spurgeon understood the importance of meditating on the word "The more you read the Bible, and the more you meditate on it, the more you will be astonished with it."

I am abiding in the Word and the Word is dwelling in me. My soul is not being dominated by what I see during the day. It's being dominated by the Word of God because I'm meditating on the Word and the Word is changing me.

There are a lot of people who miss it. They wonder why they're not having more experiences. Let me ask you some questions: What are you meditating on? What are you looking at? How are you spending your time?

If your primary focus is Facebook, YouTube, the news channel, television, your favorite movie, your favorite magazine, etc., then you will not be ascending into those high places. I am not against all that stuff, but it should be done in balance. If you want to move into the supernatural dominions, you have to train yourself to begin to focus on the unseen. You need to look at the Word of God, you need to meditate on the Word of the Lord, you need to obey the Word of God. The more you apply this spiritual exercise, the more you will change, as you embrace the mind of Christ. You have just built your own springboard to leap into the spirit realm.

KEYS TO TRANSLATING IN THE SPIRIT NUMBER THREE: FASTING

"*So we fasted and petitioned our God about this, and he answered our prayer.*"[21] Ezra prepared the Israelites to make their trek from Babylon to Jerusalem. He knew that on this journey, they would possibly be in danger from the Bedouin Arabs that prowled the desert lands. Ezra gathered the people together for fasting and prayer, seeking God's favor and protection. The fasting and prayer worked. They safely made it to Jerusalem.

Eating is a normal part of all of our lives. We begin and end the day with eating. Refraining from eating creates an interruption in the rhythm of life. However, God's people understood that this disruption brought more value to their life, the value of intimacy, communication with God, and enlisting His help. Throughout the Scriptures, fasting was a regular part of the life of Jews and Christians, from Moses to Jesus. Abstaining from food was part of the ancient culture. It certainly has not been a part of today's culture, though the importance of fasting has increased. Hopefully you can get to the place where you see fasting is not suffering, *it's feasting.*

Fasting makes your spirit more sensitive to the spiritual world around you. During times of fasting, your soul reaches a place where your spirit begins to control the soul. Too many people are dominated by their body and their soul. For those who are not born again, their spirit is disconnected from body and soul. They live in the physical world, unaware of the spiritual world.

The new creation man should be operating at all levels, spirit, soul, and body, and it is your spirit that should rule. When you are regularly praying in tongues and consistently meditating on the Word of God and fasting, your *spirit man* is strengthened and has more control over your body and soul. This opens up a great door to the spiritual realm.

One final thought on fasting. It can be helpful that you not only fast from food, but fast from television and social media. This might be harder than avoiding eating. Believe me, this is an essential part of moving into the spiritual realms I have presented to you. You should be in control of your life, not your body and soul that crave the things of the carnal life.

You want to make sure that your soul is being dominated by your spirit. What will happen as a result of this is that you will begin to have more vivid supernatural experiences. You will enter into this spiritual place where the Spirit of God will take you on a journey. The more you experience the spiritual realm, the more you will desire it. You will begin to see things that you have never seen before and you will know that there's a difference. You will notice a difference in your dreams because they will be more authentic, they will be more graphic and intense. When you begin to practice these spiritual exercises of speaking in tongues, meditating on the Word of God, and fasting, you will be surprised how spiritually aware you become.

NIGHT VISIONS

This story is a great illustration of a night vision. *The Macedonian Call,* as they refer to it, was one of the great stories in Paul's missionary travels throughout Asia and Greece and eventually parts of Western Europe. It all starts with a vision.

> "And a vision appeared to Paul in the night: a man of Macedonia was standing there, urging him and saying, 'Come over to Macedonia and help us.' And when Paul had seen the vision, immediately we sought to go on into Macedonia, concluding that God had called us to preach the gospel to them."[22]

This is a momentous event. Paul and his team were trying to push into Asia for the spreading of the Gospel. Somehow, the Holy Spirit prevented them from getting into Phrygia and Galatia. No success. They tried to get into Bithynia, but couldn't. Finally, they went down to Troas. Paul has a dream or night vision. During the night, he has a vision of a man from Macedonia with a message, "Come over to Macedonia and help us."

The theologian, Bengel, in the Pulpit Commentaries, thought it was a dream, but others thought it was a vision like Ananias had. The theologians differ between dream or vision. A couple of theologians thought the Macedonian was an angel dressed up like a Macedonian who spoke the language. There is no way to validate this. What is clear is that a Macedonian, in the middle of the night, appeared in a vision or dream, asking Paul to come over and help them. This night vision would prepare the way for the Gospel to spread to all of

Western Europe. However, concerning Asia, Paul and his team would eventually reach Asia Minor, where churches would be established in Colosse, Laodicea, Sardis, Thyatira, and Philadelphia.[23]

The next morning, Paul and his team would set sail for Troas and eventually settle in at Philippi, the first city to hear the Gospel in the West. This expansion of the Gospel would usher in the most historic event in the history of Europe, the going forth of the Word of the Lord from Jerusalem to enlighten the nations of Greece and further on to all of Europe. Paul would find great joy in preaching the Gospel in these foreign lands and bringing them into the fold of Jesus Christ.

Moving on to our study of night visions. There's a difference between dreams and night visions. Both of these are translations. Dreams are your spirit bringing things into your soul, but what happens in a night vision? In a night vision, your soul leaves this place. Your soul now joins your spirit in heavenly realms. Your soul is now controlled by your spirit. Before this, your soul was out of control.

In a night vision, you are in heavenly places in your spirit. Your soul is experiencing being seated with Christ in heavenly places. Your physical body is still on the earth. As your spirit and your soul come back down into your physical body, you begin to awaken and the glory of God from that experience you had in heaven will manifest in your body.

Let me clarify again. Your spirit is traveling. It is being translated. In other words, it is taking place in the spirit. Your spirit is bringing that information back to your soul at night. Your body is asleep. Your soul is receiving the information, but your spirit is traveling. Refresher: *your soul is your mind, will, and emotions.*

Can the soul and spirit be divided? According to the author of Hebrews, it can. *"For the word of God is quick, and powerful, and sharper than any two-edged sword, piercing even to the dividing asunder of soul and spirit, and of the joints and marrow, and is a discerner of the thoughts and intents of the heart."*[24] The only thing that can divide the soul and the spirit is the Word of God. The Word of God, which is Christ who was the Word in the beginning, has a double-edged sword, Word and

Spirit, that pierces and penetrates the soul, the very center of intellect, motives, and feelings. By the action of Word and Spirit, the soul is healed and renewed, and the spirit and soul can move together in unity.

Your spirit moves in the eternal realm or heaven. Your spirit is seated with Christ in heavenly places, according to Ephesians 2:6: *"And hath raised us up together, and made us sit together in heavenly places in Christ Jesus."* Your soul is now in a higher realm, especially when you're asleep.

Your spirit is in heavenly places while you're asleep. Your spirit is there and is impacting your imagination. That's where your dreams come in. That's where you begin to see a lot of information forming in your dreams. Your soul is now receiving and retaining the information from your spirit in the heavenly places.

Often, what will happen to you is that while you are asleep, you will have a night vision. In the middle of the night, while you are having that experience, you will wake up and your body will feel the presence of God, or the glory of God.

What happened was that your soul joined your spirit, and you brought that back down to the conscious realm of your physical body, and now you're experiencing the glory of God in the body. You're experiencing what your soul experienced while it was in heavenly places.

The glory that you are feeling on you is the glory of the impartation that you received while you were being translated, whether it was an angel, or a cloud of witnesses, or an experience, or another minister on the earth. You might hear voices or thunder. I know a lot of people who hear a door opening and closing, or they will hear knocking. What happens is that the knocking that you were hearing was the door opening, like what the Apostle John saw in the Book of Revelation.

"After this I looked, and there in heaven a door stood open!"[25]

The more that you renew your soul, the less fearful your soul will be when you begin to have these supernatural experiences. You must rid yourself of all fear. Peace is the potting soil for the presence of God. Everything will grow out of the place of peace, and you must have peace if you're going to function in the supernatural.

COUNCIL OF HEAVEN

I will conclude this chapter with some thoughts concerning the Council of the Lord. "*But who has stood in the council of the LORD, That he should see and hear His word? Who has given heed to His word and listened?*" [26]Or, look at the King James Version: "*For who has stood in the council of the Lord hath perceived and heard his word? Who hath marked his words and heard it?*"

Who has stood in the council of the Lord? Either these were the words of Jeremiah or the words of God. Whether it was Jeremiah or God, the issue is the same. The false prophets are not permitted to stand in the council of the Lord. It is His prophets and the righteous who are allowed in the council of the Lord for observation or consultation.

There are others that have their own teaching on this subject. We are talking about the same thing, but we use different languages. This is the way I received it from the Lord. Jeremiah is talking about this realm of translation here. The council of the Lord is the Seat of Christ. The council of men and angels have gathered together to hear the counsel of God.

The council of the Lord, or the *sod* of God, is a Hebrew word, meaning *a confidential, divine consultation, a circle of confidants, or council of heaven*. The prophets may sometimes be invited into the council to learn divine secrets. This process of entry into the council of the Lord is by way of translation.

Special note: When I release my book on angels, I will have deeper teaching on the Council of the Lord. Keep your eyes open for that book.

A FINAL WORD

It is meaningful to end this chapter with Isaiah's words:

> "He gives power to the weak, and to those who have no might He increases strength. But those who wait on the Lord shall renew their strength; they shall mount up with wings like eagles, they shall run and not be weary, they shall walk and not faint."[27]

This is a realm of translation. It is a progression, a training of the inexperienced. You start by waiting on the Lord. You don't get in a hurry. You wait. In the waiting process, strength is renewed. You run and you don't lose your strength. You walk and don't faint. You soar in the heavens like an eagle.

When you are entering a translation, you're pulling the spirit realm into your physical body, and your physical body experiences the glory as you are renewed. You are strengthened, you are changed, and you are transformed by the realm of heaven.

5 / TRANS-RELOCATION

THE 4 ORDERS OF SUPERNATURAL TRAVEL

THERE ARE RUMORS OF ANOTHER WORLD. I WONDER WHAT WE ARE missing. The supernatural is all around us; unfortunately, many in church are overlooking it. Above and beyond the natural world is another world, but there was a rift in the realm. When Adam and Eve became obsessed with the natural world, they lost sight of the supernatural world. The fall closed the door, for a moment.

Paul's perspective is amazing for he understands the difference between the temporal realm and the eternal realm. The rift is repaired. Our eyes are healed, and we see that which we did not see. *"While we do not look at the things which are seen, but at the things which are not seen. For the things which are seen are temporary, but the things which are not seen are eternal."* [1]

We use the word 'supernatural' often, but I am not sure how many fully understand the word. The basic Latin meaning of the word 'super' is *above, beyond, to place or be placed above or over.* The Latin word for 'above' is *super,* and thus we get the word 'supernatural.' [2] Putting it all together, supernatural is a world above and beyond the natural realm. Even that definition is not enough. Why? Because the supernatural is not just above, it is beside us.

Father John Nepil has an interesting thought that makes sense: "The Christian understanding of humanity begins in a two-fold gift in the Garden of Eden: the gift of man's existence and the gift of his sharing in the divine life. Man was created with a supernatural end."[3]

To the scientist, the word "supernatural" is a contradiction. However, the universe is natural and the supernatural is the natural not yet understood. Scientists and a lot of Christians only believe in the *normal*. They confine our world, the only world they know, to the world of natural law. The mysteries of the supernatural they have yet to explain. It is a bit hilarious since scientists have so many things that they believe in, but they cannot see. For example, proton decay has never been witnessed, and we don't know if it can even occur. However, "proton decay" is not classified as "supernatural."[4]

Paul Claudel writes, "Our God is a living God, ever new, ever in the state of being an explosion and a source, subject to no necessity arising out of that creation which he brought from nothing, a God forever inventing the heaven in which he dwells, and whose next move we can never foresee."[5] Yes, the supernatural exists, and for those who remain open, they will see.

THE GOLDEN CHAIN

I was speaking in Reading, England, and during one of the meetings, I saw a golden chain that came down into the room with a golden cross on it, and the Lord spoke to me and said, "Someone in this meeting has lost this golden chain. I want you to give it back to them." I said, "Okay, Lord, how do I do that?" He said, "Call them out by a word of knowledge."

So, I spoke the word of knowledge and said, "There's somebody here," and went through the whole scenario about the lost chain and a woman comes to the front. She spoke up, "That's my gold cross necklace. I've lost it. I haven't been able to find it." I quickly responded, "Okay, step up here."

As soon as she stepped up and I was a few feet from her, I was instantly caught away in the Spirit. I entered what I thought was a supernatural portal and, suddenly, I found myself in front of an apartment complex. You have to understand how unreal this is and how challenging it is to carry on this conversation with the lady while I go through this portal and end up at her home, all at the same time.

I share these words with the lady: "I'm standing in front of an apartment complex." The woman speaks out, "What?" I gave her the description of the apartment complex. She responds, "That's my apartment complex," and I continue with these words: "I'm going up the stairs."

Can you imagine this? Simultaneously, I'm in the Spirit and in the meeting at the same time. Back to the conversation. I say to the woman, "I'm going up the stairs. I'm going to the house number..." Then, I tell her the house number. Enthusiastically, she responds, "Oh, that's my apartment complex. That's my apartment. That's my number." I softly say, "I'm going through the door. I walked into your house." I don't remember, but the lady must have been a bit frantic at that moment.

Getting her composure, she replied, "You're going into my house." I keep the conversation going. "I'm in your house right now and you have white couches in your living room." She replied, "Oh my, you are in my house right now." I said, "I told you. I'm in your house." I take a break from the conversation with the lady and I start a conversation with God. I know it sounds bizarre, but what am I to do? I didn't start this conversation. God did. And I need some help from Him.

I ask, "Lord, where is the golden cross necklace?" He said, "Lift up the cushion and underneath the cushion on the white couch, you will find the gold cross necklace." Now, she had looked there many, many times, but it had never been there. Suddenly, I spoke out. "It's underneath the cushion in your couch at your house."

I came out of this adventure and I am back in the meeting. I tell the lady, "Go home, check underneath your couch, and on the left side, there will be the gold chain necklace." She went home that night, lifted up the couch cushion, and there it was, supernaturally. She brought it back the next night and showed it to everyone. You can watch it on YouTube at this link https://youtu.be/ei-qfNoQ2yE.

DEALING WITH THE ACCUSERS: HUMANS AND DEMONS

Before I introduce trans-relocation, I feel compelled to share with you things that you will encounter as you go deeper into the supernatural.

When I am speaking about supernatural travel, I always feel the necessity of laying a strong scriptural foundation. I am preparing the way for you to handle the accusers who will come your way. There will be times when someone will tell you that your teaching is demonic. They will insist that there is no scriptural reference for teachings on the supernatural. You will notice that every topic I preach on is always backed up and founded upon the Scriptures.

When your foundation is on the Word, you are secure, and you will be able to combat humans and demons. The devil is sly and will tell you anything to get you to doubt what you believe. The deceiver will tell you that you are in deception and are no longer following the ways of the Lord. There will be those moments when someone will say that anything related to the supernatural is demonic. They think they are doing you a favor, but they are not. They deny what they have not experienced and what they have not studied in the Scriptures. Most of these people are only repeating what others have said. They have no foundation for what they speak.

One of the keys to building a solid foundation is the Laws of the Spirit. God has established certain laws that apply in the natural world and the spiritual world. As there are fixed laws in our world, so there are laws in the spiritual world. Like any other law of creation, it is real, verifiable, and dependable. The Law of the Spirit is a spiritual law describing a spiritual reality. *"For the law of the Spirit of life in Christ Jesus has made me free from the law of sin and death."*[6] I like how this verse is unraveled by John Gill's Exposition: "It may be called the law, or doctrine of the Spirit, because the Spirit is the author of it, and makes it powerful and effectual to the good of souls; by it the Spirit of God is conveyed into the heart. The substance of it are spiritual things."[7]

These laws are unchangeable. They are not new laws; they have always existed. Therefore, whoever is moving in the Spirit has to operate in accordance with these laws. Satan is not a creator. He has created nothing. He's a fallen angel. Satan did not create the supernatural. He only mimics it, manipulates it, and brings deception into it.

There are those Christian circles who have gone wrong by labeling certain manifestations as being demonic simply because they believe that miracles stopped at the end of the apostolic age, as they define it. Humans cannot define or determine what the law of the Spirit will be, nor can Satan or the fallen angels. Humans and demons do not get to make the rules.

Gravity is a natural law, except when God chooses to violate His own created law. Consider this verse again, concerning Ezekiel: *"He put out the form of a hand and took me by a lock of my head, and the Spirit lifted me up between earth and heaven."*[8] Then, there is Enoch, Elijah, some of the prophets, and Jesus. All of them experienced being lifted up into spiritual realms.

One of the great laws of God is the law of the blood. We have no access to the Spirit except by the blood of the Lamb. The blood of Jesus gives us access to His glorious life. Here are some verses to consider and then we will continue.

"But now in Christ Jesus you who once were far off have been brought near by the blood of Christ." (Ephesians 2:13)

"And they overcame him by the blood of the Lamb, and by the word of their testimony, and they loved not their lives unto death." (Revelation 12:11)

"Therefore, brethren, having boldness to enter the Holiest by the blood of Jesus, by a new and living way which He consecrated for us, through the veil, that is, His flesh, and having a High Priest over the house of God, let us draw near with a true heart in full assurance of faith, having our hearts sprinkled from an evil conscience and our bodies washed with pure water." (Hebrews 10:19-22)

By the power of the blood, we experience life, we are brought near to the spiritual realm, we overcome the enemy, and we can enter into the holy place, the secret place of the Almighty. In the Old Testament, the priest had to sprinkle blood before entrance could be made by the Spirit. *"The priest shall dip his finger in the blood and sprinkle some of the blood seven times before the LORD, in front of the veil of the sanctuary."*[9] This sacrifice became a type and shadow of the real sacrifice made by Christ. It was a law for them to enter into the Spirit. As Ephesians 2:1 says, *"We have been brought near by the blood of the lamb."* The author of Hebrews offers these awesome words found in Hebrews 10:19: *"...boldness to enter the Holiest by the blood of Jesus, by a new and living way."* By the blood of Christ, we are brought near into the holiest place, into the realm of the glory and the Spirit of God. How do they go into the Spirit realm? It is by the blood that we are qualified to enter into the heavenly realm.

By the blood of the Lamb and the authority of the Spirit, we take authority over the demonic realm. They might offer up sacrifices, but the blood is ineffectual because it is the blood of animals and not the blood of Christ. The Law of the Spirit doesn't change. There is only one door and that is the door of the blood of Christ and the guidance of the Holy Spirit.

THE HEAVENLY CALL

Before I share the three keys to trans-relocation, I have a story that is found in the book, *The Heavenly Man*, by Brother Yun (one of my heroes in the faith). This is his story:

I began to wait on the Lord for his guidance, and a wonderful thing happened. One night around 10 p.m. – before my parents had gone to bed – I had just completed a time of prayer and had memorized Acts chapter 12. As I lay down on my bed, I suddenly felt someone tap my shoulder and heard a voice tell me, "Yun, I am going to send you to the West and South to be my witness." Thinking it was my mother speaking, I jumped out of my bed and went to my parents' room. I asked her, "Did you call my name? Who tapped me on my shoulder?"

My mother said, "Neither of us called for you. Go back to sleep." I prayed again and climbed into bed. Thirty minutes after again lying down I heard a clear voice that urged me, "Yun, you shall go to the West and to the South to proclaim the gospel. You shall be my witness and will testify on behalf of my name."

Immediately I got up and told my mother what had happened. She told me to go back to sleep and asked me not to be so excited. She was concerned I was losing my mind again! I knelt down and prayed to the Lord, "Jesus, if you're speaking to me, then I am listening. If you're calling me to preach your good news, then I'm willing to obey your call on my life."

Around four o'clock the next morning I received a dream from the Lord. I saw the same loving old man who had given me the bread in my previous vision. As he walked towards me, he looked into my eyes and said, "You should face the West and South to proclaim the gospel and be the Lord's witness."

In my dream I also saw a large meeting with a multitude of people. The old man radiated great authority before the crowd. He told me, "You shall be my witness to them." I felt inadequate. In the meeting a demon-possessed woman came toward me. The old man said, "You should lay your hands on her and cast the demon out in Jesus' name." In the dream I did so. The woman struggled as if she was in the throes of death. Then she was completely set free from the demonic forces that controlled her. All the people were amazed because they had never seen such things before.

Suddenly in my dream a young man came out of the crowd and asked, "Are you Brother Yun? Our brothers and sisters have been fasting and praying for you for three days. We hope you will come to our midst and preach the gospel to us. We desperately need you to come to our village." The young man told me his name, age, and home village. I was moved and told him, "I shall go to your place tomorrow." At daybreak I hurriedly called my parents and told them I was going to preach the gospel because Jesus Christ had commanded me to do so. My mother asked me where I intended to go. I told her, "Last night the Lord spoke to me three times. He told me, 'Go West and South to preach the gospel.' I will be obedient to the heavenly call."[10]

Brother Yung was only 16 at the time of this story. According to his word, he left for the West where he met a young man waiting for him. In Gao Village, there was a great revival, all because of the dream and the Gao Village Call (sort of like the Macedonian Call). Brother Yung would go on to meet the man in his dream and would head to the South where revival continued.

TRANS-RELOCATION

Trans-relocation is when your body, soul, and spirit are transported to another place in the spirit. As a refresher, the first order of supernatural travel is translation, which is when you are moving something from one place to the other, but only in the Spirit.

Our first introduction to trans-relocation is found in Hebrews 11:5: "*By faith Enoch was translated that he should not see death; and was not found, because God had translated him: for before his translation he had this testimony, that he pleased God.*" Enoch did not have some kind of unique anointing; there was not a glory given to Enoch that allowed him to trans-relocate. There was one thing that set Enoch apart from others: he had a testimony that *he pleased God.*

In the dry catalog of ancient times, a jewel was found, a man who deeply loved God and brought delight to Him. His reward was that God took him home. He was trans-relocated, bypassing mortality straight into the arms of Father God. There are four keys to trans-relocation: faith, the Spirit of the Lord, no fear, and love. It seems that these four always make it into every list of keys for serving God.

THE FIRST KEY: FAITH

It is easy to quickly become obsessed with the translation part of the verse, and why not? There are not many who skipped mortality and went straight through the gates of heaven. Maybe it was because of those 300 years of walking with God that influenced God's decision to take Enoch home.

In spite of his glorious relocation, there was a reason why he was chosen by God to quickly move to the other side of life here on earth. *"By faith Enoch was translated that he should not see death."* After three centuries of spiritual intimacy, he was not. He was relocated to heaven's home. Faith is the key. We know that without faith, it is impossible to please God, and Enoch certainly found favor with God.

Pleasing God is the key to opening the door to trans-relocation. The principle of the law of trans-relocation is faith. It doesn't operate any other way. Whenever you hear of some amazing story of supernatural travel, you can be assured that the person pleased God and walked by faith. It wasn't because of his theology or his preaching or his special gifts. It was simple. It was his faith in God. It is certainly good for all of us who are just ordinary people to trust Him and desire His presence.

The Scriptures did not mention his anointing, nor did the subject of the glory come into the conversation. This does not minimize the anointing and the glory. Those are certainly keys to ministry, but they are not keys to the supernatural.

When we are discussing trans-relocation, we're talking about your body, your soul, and your spirit being caught up, transported, and trans-relocated into another place. These types of manifestations always begin in faith.

THE SECOND KEY: THE SPIRIT OF THE LORD

When I refer to trans-relocation, I have in mind the catching up of the total person, including spirit, soul and body. There is another biblical story that relates to trans-relocation. It is the story of Philip. *"Now when they came up out of the water, the Spirit of the Lord caught Philip away, so that the eunuch saw him no more; and he went on his way rejoicing."*[11]

The second key is the Spirit of the Lord. Before we address the story of Philip, it is rather essential that we understand the story of the Ethiopian Eunuch. Philip had already opened the gospel door to the Samaritans and now he would have the opportunity to touch Africa. An angel appears and tells Philip to head toward the desert lands of Gaza. Jewish influence had already reached Ethiopia and it is rather certain that the Ethiopian Eunuch was influenced by Judaism. He had great power because he was in the first rank of the queen and in charge of the treasury. One didn't have to guess that he was a eunuch because most leaders in the court of the queen were eunuchs. Being a eunuch would not allow him access into the Jewish courts, though he was received as a follower of the Jewish faith. He was on his way to Jerusalem to worship.

The Spirit told Philip to quickly join the Ethiopian on his chariot. Philip quickly joined the Ethiopian and engaged him in deep conversation starting with the Old Testament Scriptures and ended up preaching Jesus to this man.

"Philip had already shared the message of Jesus with the Samaritans. Now God expanded the community to include not just Ethiopian descendants of Solomon's royal line, but a man who had been formally excluded from worshiping in the temple because of being a eunuch. Philip helped expand the understanding of who was part of God's beloved community."[12] At this point, the Ethiopian was ready to accept Christ and be baptized. After the baptism, Philip is trans-relocated, caught up to another place, and the eunuch saw him no more. Benson Commentary offers his perspective on Philips' experience, which would confirm my position on trans-relocation: "Namely, in a miraculous manner, probably transporting him, part of the way at least, through the air; a thing which seems to have happened with respect to some of the prophets."[13]

Once Philip has completed his assignment, the Spirit of the Lord trans-relocates him and he is found in Azotus, about 30 miles from Gaza.

Concerning the Spirit of the Lord, let's redirect to Isaiah 11:1-2:

"A shoot will come up from the stump of Jesse; from his roots a

Branch will bear fruit. The Spirit of the Lord will rest on him—the Spirit of wisdom and of understanding, the Spirit of counsel and of might, the Spirit of the knowledge and fear of the Lord—and he will delight in the fear of the Lord."

The Spirit of the Lord is seven distinct manifestations of the nature of the Holy Spirit. The Spirit of the Lord, the Spirit of wisdom, the Spirit of understanding, the Spirit of counsel, the Spirit of might, the Spirit of knowledge, and the Spirit of the fear of the Lord.

The seven Spirits open the door to trans-relocation, and the real key is that the Spirit of the Lord must rest upon you as stated in Isaiah. It is my experience that many times when people begin to first enter into this realm, they do it while they are asleep. Why? Because there is an element of resting that is involved in supernatural translation. Supernatural experiences can be exhausting, and it is important to find your rest in the Spirit of the Lord.

Each one of the seven Spirits of the Lord have a particular function, color, sound, vibration, and frequency. When the Spirit of the Lord is resting upon you, the power of God will often cause you to be trans-relocated.

"*The Spirit of the Lord is upon me because He has anointed me to preach the gospel to the poor. He has sent me to heal the broken heart and to preach deliverance to the captives, recovery of sight to the blind, to set at liberty them that are bruised, to preach the acceptable year of the Lord.*" [14]This is the mission statement of Jesus. Throughout His life, He was anointed and had one supreme desire, and that was to preach the gospel to the poor. The ministry of Jesus has included trans-relocation. Establishing that point we move to verses 28-31:

"So all those in the synagogue, when they heard these things, were filled with wrath, and rose up and thrust Him out of the city; and they led Him to the brow of the hill on which their city was built, that they might throw Him down over the cliff. Then passing through the midst of them, He went His way. Then He went down to

Capernaum, a city of Galilee, and was teaching them on the Sabbaths."

Jesus' audience wanted special favors because He was in His hometown. They came to see the miracles He performed. It wasn't quite the show they had hoped for. The atmosphere of the crowd turned from curious people to an angry and murderous crowd. They wanted a miracle, and Jesus did an unexpected one right in front of them, escaping miraculously. Most of the time, I find that the majority of theologians will be authentic and candid in their research, but not with this event in the life of Jesus. They could not accept the miracle that was before their very eyes, but it was a miracle. How was Jesus able to escape from the clutches of this angry mob? We are told the answer. It is obviously clear. He passed through their midst. A miracle happened. Jesus experienced a trans-relocation to Capernaum. He passed through because the Spirit of the Lord was resting upon Him. He experienced the same miracle that happened to Philip.

Did God only have one uniquely begotten Son? Hebrews answers that question in a very obvious way. "*For it became Him, for whom are all things, and by whom are all things, in bringing many sons unto glory, to make the captain of their salvation perfect through sufferings.*"[15]

Jesus died and shed His blood so that He could bring many sons into glory. You are a son and you have the same access to supernatural power that Jesus had as written in Luke 4. It doesn't matter what demonic spirit tries to come against you, when you decree and declare the Word of the Lord. The Spirit of the Lord will rest upon you and you will receive revelation, and when it is timely, the Spirit of the Lord will trans-relocate you by the power of God.

This is the final verse we will look at before moving on to the next key. "*And it shall come to pass, as soon as I am gone from thee, that the Spirit of the LORD shall carry thee whither I know not; and so when I come and tell Ahab, and he cannot find thee, he shall slay me: but I thy servant fear the LORD from my youth.*"[16]

This is another example in the Old Testament of the Spirit of the

Lord resting upon someone and carrying them to another place or causing them to miraculously pass through a crowd as Jesus did. The seven Spirits were in process. The theologians got their thinking cap back on and were able to see that this was a miracle. This is the Pulpit Commentaries' theological evaluation: "Such a transportation must have already occurred in the history of Elijah, but the sudden, mysterious disappearance and the long concealment of the prophet is quite unusual."[17]

Elijah's servant could fluctuate back and forth at times for fear of the king. In this case, he stood with Elijah. The servant speaks up and tells Elijah, "Look, you want me to go tell Ahab that you're here? But I know that the Spirit of the Lord is going to carry you away, and you will pass through the supernatural realm. I'm not going to be able to find you." Elijah had the Spirit of the Lord upon him and he also had faith and was carried away.

THE THIRD KEY: NO FEAR

This is where it gets very interesting. Buckle up. We are ready to launch into supernatural territory.

> "And when even was now come, his disciples went down unto the sea, And entered into a ship, and went over the sea toward Capernaum. And it was now dark, and Jesus was not coming to them. And the sea arose by reason of a great wind that blew. So when they had rowed about five and twenty or thirty furlongs, they saw Jesus walking on the sea, and drawing nigh unto the ship: and they were afraid. But he saith unto them, It is I; be not afraid. Then they willingly received him into the ship: and immediately the ship was at the land whither they went." [18]

You will find out that not only can people be trans-relocated, so can *things*. It would be good for you to understand that the universe is alive. Everything is vibrating, functioning, and making a sound and a vibrational frequency. There's life in all matter, whether it's a solid, a liquid, plasma, gas, no matter what it may seem to be, everything is living.

I will dissect this so I can give you a spiritual viewpoint on this story of trans-relocation. The story starts with the disciples reluctantly getting into their boat and heading out to sea toward Capernaum. They were not too keen on leaving the Master. It was close to nightfall and they had gone out about three to five miles. Their natural course toward Capernaum would have been almost parallel with the shore. Darkness was setting in; the sea was rising, and Jesus had not yet come.

There were twelve men in the boat. Excuse me, make it thirteen since Jesus got in the boat, *eventually*. The boat was not some kind of small boat in the middle of the sea and three to five miles out. Peter, James, and John were professional fishermen, so the boat had to be quite large. Consider one of those Grecian ships and that will give you an idea of what size it could be. Maybe not huge, but it was a very big ship.

Jesus is now drawing near to the ship, walking on the water. Before we consider the fearful disciples, we have to talk about Jesus walking on water. You have to admit that Christ is Lord of the material universe. By His almighty power, He fused the waves into compliance to support His material body while walking on the waters. There was no problem for Jesus. This is a manifestation of the glory of Christ and His power over the physical order of things. "This is a wonderful picture which is true for all ages of the mighty Christ, to whose gentle footfall the unquiet surges are as a marble pavement; and who draws near in the purposes of His love, and using even opposing forces as the path for His triumphant progress."[19]

The disciples are frightened as Jesus approaches them in the boat. Jesus is aware of their terrified hearts and says, "Be not afraid."

Here is your third key. If you are going to be trans-relocated, you cannot be afraid. You cannot work in fear. I'll keep reiterating that. You have to cast away all your fear.

You must trust the Lord with everything. If you ask Him for a fish, will He give you a serpent?[20] Of course not. He does not play games with His children. If your earthly father knows how to give good gifts, how much more does our heavenly Father know how to give us good gifts?[21] As long as you have fear, you will never be able to enter into faith and the Spirit of the Lord can never give you rest. *"For the Spirit which God has given us is not a spirit of cowardice, but one of power and of love and of sound judgment."*[22]

They had fought valiantly through the night with the thunderous squalls blowing across the lake. As the light of dawn broke over the eastern waters, something approached them. Their hearts freeze with fear at the figure approaching them, walking on water. The closer this thing gets to them, they finally realize that this figure is none other than Jesus.

Fear operates out of darkness. If you are desirous of experiencing the supernatural, or an inanimate object comes toward you, or if you are trans-relocated, you cannot operate in fear. You must operate in the flame of faith and courage, not the darkness of doubt and fear.

Jesus was not afraid for He operated with the mind of God. He understood the depths of spiritual realities and the world of quantum physics before it was ever discovered. He understood that He could transcend the laws of the natural universe. Jesus understood that He could not only trans-locate His disciples, but He could do the same with their entire ship. Besides that, even the seas recognized Him as Lord and would obey His every command.

All the world is waiting for you to release life upon it. You will speak to things that aren't near you and they will trans-relocate to you, because everything is trans-dimensional. Whatever your need is, it can be supplied supernaturally, if you believe. But you must cast out fear and embrace faith.

When you understand that not only can you or a group of people be trans-relocated into heaven, or in a different geographical location, but also inanimate objects can be trans-relocated, you are now beginning to understand dimensions of the Spirit. When you are moving in high dimensions of glory, you move outside of the paradigm of religion and tradition and you begin to move into new places and frontiers. There are realms of glory that God wants you and me to enter into.

A TRANS-RELOCATION EXPERIENCE

I had just come back from a trip to the nation of Brazil and I was driving down the road with my wife Brynn and my son, who was three at the time. Nehemiah, my son, was in the back seat, Brynn was in the passenger's seat, and I was driving. We were driving down a very well-known section in Nashville and moving into Smyrna where we lived at the time.

As we were traveling, we reached a place called Bell Road. It's an intersection, and we were chatting profusely. I was talking with Brynn about the Book of Revelation. As I was driving, I asked Brynn to turn to the Book of Revelation. Without any delay, she opened the Book of Revelation and started reading about the seven churches of Revelation.

> "Unto the church, unto the angel of the church of Ephesus write these things He who holds the seven stars in his right hand, who walks in the midst of the seven golden candlesticks. I know that works, thy labor, thy patience, and how thou cannot bear them which are evil. Thou hast tried them, which say they are apostles and they are not. They're found to be liars. Though I was born as patience, and for my name's sake, you labored and has not fainted. Nevertheless, I have something against thee, thou hast left thy first love. Remember, therefore, when thou art has fallen, repent and do the first works. So, come to thee and remove the candlestick from out of place except thou repent."[23]

Brynn continues reading while I am driving. We are going through a certain section called Bell Road. Suddenly, these little lights started shooting in the car. I look at Brynn and ask, "Honey, do you see that?" And she responds fervently, "Wow, what is that?" Though we were distracted, suddenly, we find ourselves in the car coming back down the hill through the exact same intersection, Bell Road, once again.

We had been trans-relocated in the car—my wife, myself, and my son Nehemiah—while Brynn was reading the verses in Revelation. It was so shocking that my son started shouting from the back seat saying, "Daddy, daddy, daddy, we've already been here before. Why are we coming back to this place? We've already been here!" He didn't know the word, but he did know that we had been trans-relocated.

I pulled over on the side of the road. I was trying to make sense of what had just happened, and the Spirit of the Lord spoke to me and said, "Charlie, do you want to move in greater power?" I said, "Yes, Lord." He said, "Do you not just want to speak to the pastor or the congregation of churches, but do you want to speak to the angel of the church?" The Lord continued to speak to me and said, "Notice how Paul wrote letters to churches and pastors, but John entered into a greater dimension where he was not speaking to pastors. He was speaking to the angels of the church, a higher dimension." I said, "Yes, Lord."

Continuing, the Lord said, "I'm ringing a bell, a clear bell to this generation that if they are to trans-relocate or move in the Spirit in any capacity, they must learn how to love."

THE FOURTH KEY: LOVE

Love is the fourth key to moving in trans-relocation. If you can't love people, you can't move in trans-relocation, because everything, every supernatural thing, is determined by this element of love. *"You shall love the Lord your God with all your heart, with all your soul, and with all your mind. This is the first and great commandment. And the second is like it: You shall love your neighbor as yourself. On these two commandments hang all the Law and the Prophets."*[24]

In their ethical teaching, many had secured the scholarly truth but had not seized the spirit of the law. They maintained the canons of the faith and were enthusiastic in resisting the sponsors of sin. But they had lost their first love.

The spirit of love is what gives value to the law. The Jews built a fence around the original law, a fence that was composed of six hundred and thirteen laws. Their love had abated in its fervency of holy love.

The words of Jesus made LOVE to be the supreme law. May that love for God and man be pure, hearty, and sincere. Brotherly love is a positive and authentic proof of the faith. You shall love God and man with all the powers of your faculties. If you're not willing to crucify your flesh and love people, you will never see this operate in your life. In contradiction to the praise given to the Ephesian church for their labor, patience, and discernment, the Lord had something negative to say: "*You have lost your first love.*" The decay of love is the decay of all graces.

The city of Ephesus was the center for a cultism in the entire Asian province. This city had the temple dedicated to Diana. Unfortunately, there was a temporary decline in the Ephesian church, after Paul's departure. But under the leadership of the followers of John, the teachings of the Apostle Paul were resurrected, and love returned with great passion. Eventually, Ephesus became the most prominent center of Christianity in the East.

Do you want to move in power and in the supernatural? Then, clothe yourself with love. If you don't learn how to love, you'll never enter into the right door, the door of life, and sweet spirituality. You have wandered and wonder how to find your way back.

"Prone to wander, Lord, I feel it;

Prone to leave the God I love:

Take my heart, oh, take and seal it

With Thy Spirit from above."[25]

"*Remember therefore from where you* have fallen; *repent and do the works you did at first.*" The door is not locked, and the story is not over. Remember your first love and repent and return to the place of love for God and for others.

All it takes is a supernatural moment that will renew your love and mend your apathy. That one moment where the Lord trans-relocated me and my three-year old son and Brynn on Bell Road changed my life forever. I recognized that if I did not grow in love, I would not see the full potential of the supernatural life. If I could not love people in a greater way, and I could not love the Lord in a greater way, then I would never experience more of the heavenly realm.

Where people so often go wrong in their exercise of the supernatural is when they become obsessed with the supernatural but not passionate about loving God and people. The more possessed they are with supernatural things and the more successful they become for spiritual realms and supernatural experiences, the quicker they will deviate from the love for God and others. This path could quickly lead you toward the pathway of pride and arrogance. Many have fallen, traveling along those dark alleys. The path of pride will eventually lead you to the darkness of deception.

Do not fear the places of the supernatural and the heavenly realms. But your first and primary focus must be intimacy with Jesus and love for people. If you want to be trans-relocated in your body, in your soul, in your spirit, then do it for the love of others and so you can help them.

Henri Nouwen, a Dutch Roman Catholic priest, was one of the most beloved and important spiritual writers of the twentieth century. He was well-known as one who loved others, greatly. These words express that love: "Often we speak about love as if it is a feeling. But if we wait for a feeling of love before loving, we may never learn to love well. The feeling of love is beautiful and life-giving, but our loving cannot be based on that feeling. To love is to think, speak, and act according to the spiritual knowledge that we are infinitely loved by God and called to make that love visible in this world. In our world of loneliness and despair, there is an enormous need for men and women who know the heart of God, a heart that forgives, that cares, that reaches out and wants to heal."[26]

There is the love of God's power and there is the power of God's love.

6 / BILOCATION

THE 4 ORDERS OF SUPERNATURAL TRAVEL

TOWARD THE END OF HIS LIFE, ALBERT EINSTEIN WAS ASKED IF HE HAD any regrets. He answered, "I wish I had read more of the mystics earlier in my life." This is a significant confession, coming from one of the greatest geniuses of the 20th century. Added to the thoughts of Einstein are the words of Carl Jung, the psychiatrist and philosopher: "Only the mystics bring what is creative to religion itself."[1]

What is mysticism? The descriptions would range from the view of Christians to New Agers and Buddhists. Even among the Christians, there would be a diversity of definitions and an exposition of experiences. C.S. Lewis had his own definition for mysticism: "Christian Mysticism is the direct experience of God, immediate as a taste or color." In his book, *Pursuit of God*, A.W. Tozer describes it this way: "A mystic is a believer who practices the presence of God" (I think he borrowed that from Brother Lawrence, smiling).[2]

A mystic is someone who desires union with God and actively maintains that union through prayer and contemplation. Carl McColman has a sweet description: "*Mysticism* implies not legalistic religion, but living spirituality — heart-felt intimacy with God, centered on a miraculous and joyful appreciation of the Spirit's ability to heal and transform lives."[3] Union with God, when miraculously unveiled, is a multiplicity of spiritual experiences such as spiritual ecstasies, visions, levitations, angelic encounters, and other supernatural encounters. Mysticism's primary focus is the search for an inward, immediate experience of God that will lead to varied mystical, supernatural experiences, often similar to the mystical experiences in the Old and New Testament. Union with God, at times, can position you so close to God and the heavenly realm that it is difficult for the mystic to remain on earth, desiring to be more fully united with their ultimate love.

In our times, there is a growing desire for a much deeper relationship with God, accompanied with passion to experience the supernatural realms of heavenly reality. This company of Christians is craving for genuine spirituality, and they are cynical of and disappointed with legalistic, controlling religion and the acidic and empty culture around us.

Unfortunately, many in the group of fundamentalist and left-brained anti-supernatural liberals distort mysticism and its supernatural experiences. Because they do not understand the mystic way, they are quick to define them as a cult of New Agers, witches, and Buddhists.

In spite of that cluster of cynics, I sense that most humans yearn for an intimate union with God that will take them beyond the ordinary. Amongst the company of mystics, there is a deep desire in the heart for what feels like the unattainable. They search for something more. Is it there? It will be found in the inner exploration of their soul and the guidance of the Holy Spirit, who will lead them to the supernatural realms they long to encounter. These words of Evelyn Underhill in her classic book, *Mystics of the Church*, ring true: "The mystic's heart beats in union with God's heart, so 'the heart's desire' is God's desire." As St. John of the Cross said, "Launch out into the deep."

Before moving into the revelation and stories of bilocation, I want to finish up the story of the mystics with this observation. The mystics could be defined as a variety of different communities, with different centers of focus. I will define these centers in three remarkable ways. All three of them are dissimilar, but akin to each other in many ways. The differences are found in their unique emphasis. The borders are not fixed but flexible. The mystics long for a life beyond tedious routine and lifeless religion. They searched for a union with God so that they could not find any distinction between them and God.

Union: the true goal of the mystic quest. The company associated with mystical union claims that the soul may be lifted into a union with God so close and so complete that it is merged into the being of God. The whole life of man is a return journey to God: he came from God and must go back to Him. This classic quote by St. Augustine is embraced by those who seek total harmony with God: "Thou hast made us for Thyself, O Lord, and our heart is restless until it rests in Thee."

Mystics: St. Teresa of Avila, St. John of the Cross, Madame Guyon, Bernard of Clairvaux, Evelyn Underhill, Ruysbroeck, Eckhart, Francois Fenelon, Thomas a Kempis, Michael Molinos, and others.

They believed in and longed for total union with God. "When Jesus is near," wrote Thomas a Kempis, "all is well, and nothing seems difficult. When He is absent, all is hard. When Jesus does not speak within, all other comfort is empty, but if He says only a word, it brings great consolation." Thus, our soul yearns for nearness. It is the yearning inclination of the soul that seeks total union with God. St. Francis de Sales expressed union with God in his poetic language, *"The magnet draws iron and holds it fast to itself; Lord Jesus, my Beloved, be the magnet of my heart: draw, hold fast, unite forever my spirit to Your paternal heart! Oh, since I was made for You, how is it that I am not in You?"*[4]

Finally, Evelyn Underhill, born in the 1800s, was a renowned author on Christian mysticism and identified five steps to mystical union, a process that is common to all those who followed the mystic way. During the awakening process, the seeker becomes aware of something supernatural and that awareness creates an intense hunger for God. The second stage, purgative, is the process of a stripping away of their imperfections and abandoning all for Christ. The third stage is the stage of illumination, where spiritual reality meets. The light of heaven shines and is often accompanied with ecstatic moments. The fourth stage is the dark night of the soul (a poetic work of St. John of the Cross), preludes the fourth stage which is called the Unitive way. It is during this final stage where the beloved is united with her lover in a transforming union. This transforming union accompanied by a beatific vision where the mystic sees Jesus Christ in a face to face encounter.

These mystics have experienced mysticism so fervently that when they "come back down to earth," they can start to have what we refer to as "withdrawal symptoms" of God's presence. The final stage is that the seeker has reached the place of mystic union with God. Their union is so complete and real that they now have become a liaison between things on earth and things in the eternal realms.[5]

It is possible that most readers will not be aware of the Mystical Union. It would be my desire for you to join their company and find your way to that blessed union with God. Once there, I hope you will also experience *withdrawal symptoms* of God's presence.

By the way, all of these mystics mentioned in this section had incredible supernatural experiences of ecstasy, visions, and miracles.

ACTIVIST MYSTICS

This is the path where activism meets mysticism and one gives birth to the other. This is not a new phenomenon. Here are four characteristics that illustrate the *Activist Prophets*.

It starts with the Mystics and the Prophets. There is no debating the mystical experiences of the prophets. "Surely the Lord GOD does nothing, unless He reveals His secret to His servants the prophets."[6] Elijah rides on a flying chariot of fire, Ezekiel is shown the glory and the throne of God, and Isaiah is shown future events. This is only a snippet of the supernatural experiences of the prophets.

In his book, *The Prophetic Imagination*, Walter Brueggerman reveals a different side of the mystic prophets: the activists. "The task of prophetic ministry is to nurture, nourish, and evoke a consciousness and perception alternative to the consciousness and perception of the dominant culture around us."[7] The prophets were the resistance force to the unrestrained power of tyrannical kings. In confronting the ruling powers, they spoke for the weak, the oppressed, the disenfranchised—those who had little voice in shaping their own lives or their own future.

The way of Jesus is both mystical and social. Jesus is well known for His miracles. Jesus walked on water, healed the blind, fed the multitudes, trans-located out of the reach of an angry crowd, and raised the dead. However, there is the other side of Jesus. He embodied prophetic spirituality where He welcomed the marginalized, affirmed women, associated with the lepers, and reached out to the poor and disowned. Jesus confronted the social structures of His day. Jesus was constantly the proverbial *pain in the side* of the religious leaders, by denouncing Pharisees, arguing with the scribes, eating meals with prostitutes, and overturning the temple tables.

As a young girl, Catherine of Siena often went to a cave near her home to meditate, fast, and pray. At about age 7, she had a vision of Jesus with Peter, Paul, and John the Evangelist; she then announced to her parents her determination to live a life dedicated to Christ. "Catherine was not satisfied living a contemplative life; she wanted to help the poor and sick. Catherine began an active ministry to the poor, the sick, and the imprisoned of Siena. When a wave of the plague struck her hometown in 1374, most people fled, but she and her followers stayed to nurse the ill and bury the dead. She was said to be tireless by day and night, healing all of whom the physicians despaired; some even claimed she raised the dead. In a series of letters, Catherine exhorted the pope to address the problems of the church and charged him to return to Rome: 'Respond to the Holy Spirit who is calling you! I tell you: Come! Come! Come! Don't wait for time because time isn't waiting for you.'"[8]

The final Mystic Activist we will review is Howard Thurman. Thurman was born in 1899 and died in 1981. He was a Baptist preacher, theologian, and the first African American dean of a traditionally white American university and founder of the first interracial interfaith congregation in the United States. Thurman had two major influences in his life: the Quaker mystic, Rufus Jones, and the civil rights activist, Martin Luther King. It was Thurman who deeply influenced King with the ways of the mystic.

Thurman declared that the mystic should not escape the turmoil of life, but has the mandate to be God's companion in promoting God's vision "on earth as it is in heaven." In 1949, Thurman published his best-selling book, *Jesus and the Disinherited*. These words express the activist side of his mystic soul: "*It cannot be denied that too often the weight of the Christian movement has been on the side of the strong and the powerful and against the weak and oppressed—this, despite the gospel.*"[9]

Thurman saw that trouble was on every side: extreme political divisiveness and abuse, racial prejudice, injustice with women's rights, religious conflict, poverty, and homelessness. In Thurman's lectures on "Mysticism and Social Action," he defined mysticism as "the response of the individual to a personal encounter with God within his own soul. Such a response is total, affecting the inner quality of the life and its outward expression as its manifestation."[10] In the spirit of his teacher, Quaker professor and spiritual guide Rufus Jones, Thurman proclaimed an "affirmative mysticism," which saw God moving through our social structures, as well as personal experience seeking the spiritual and interpersonal unity of all things.

Thurman believed that "...for the mystic, social action is sacramental, because it is not an end in itself. Always, it is the individual who must be addressed, located and released, underneath his misery and his hunger and his destitution. Whatever may be blocking his way to his own center where his altar may be found, this must be removed."[11]

TRAVELING MYSTICS

We conclude this tripartite exploration of the mystic way. The desire was to create for you a broader view of the experiences and passions of the mystics. This third path of the mystics leads you to my personal revelation and experiences in the Four Orders of Supernatural Travel.

Translation is the very first order of supernatural travel. What do I mean by translation? Translation is the process of moving something or someone to another place, from earth to heaven, or from one place on earth to another. In this case, it is only by the spirit, not the physical body. It's just your spirit traveling.

Trans-relocation is when your body, soul, and spirit are transported to another place in the spirit. There are four keys to trans-relocation: faith, the Spirit of the Lord, no fear, and love. It seems that these four always make it into every list of keys for serving God. This chapter will be followed up with the other two ways of supernatural travel: bilocation and transfiguration.

Bilocation is the miraculous ability where a person or thing will be located in two different places at the same time.

Our final word on the *traveling mystics*, supernatural travel, is *transfiguration*. Transfiguration is a complete change in your form or appearance into a more beautiful, spiritual state.

PADRE PIO SAVES A CITY

The story of Padre Pio is my first story of those who experienced bilocation. Padre Pio was a priest and mystic who was venerated as a saint in the Catholic Church. The phenomenon of bilocation was one of the amazing gifts attributed to Padre Pio.

His stories are quite amazing. I will share with you two wonderful stories. One day, a former Italian Army Officer entered the sacristy and was watching the padre. Suddenly he said, "Yes, here he is. I am not wrong." He approached Padre Pio and, kneeling in front of him crying, he said, "Padre, thank you for saving me from death." Afterward, the man told the people present there, "I was a Captain of the Infantry and one day on the battlefield in a terrible hour of battle, not far from me I saw a friar who said, 'Sir, go away from that place!' I went towards him and as soon as I moved, a grenade burst in the place where I was before and opened a chasm. I turned around in order to find the friar, but he was not there anymore." Padre Pio, who was bilocating, had saved his life.[12]

The most remarkable documented cases of bilocation were Padre Pio's appearance in the air over San Giovanni Rotondo during World War II. While Southern Italy was still in the hands of the Nazis, American bombers were given the task of bombing the city. Upon hearing of this possibility, he went to church to pray. He knelt down and prayed fervently. Padre Pio promised his people that the city would never be bombed.

An American pilot was just about to bomb the city when, "Suddenly, the pilot saw in front of his plane the image of a monk in the sky, gesturing with his arms and hands for the plane to turn back. The shocked pilot did just that and jettisoned his bombs elsewhere. When he returned to the base and told his story, his commanding officer decided it was best to put this pilot in a hospital under observation for mission-fatigue."[13] God had supernaturally lifted up Friar Pio into the air while he was still praying in the church. All attempts to release the bombs failed. His prayers saved the city as he promised the citizens. It was the only city in Italy that was not bombed.

The pilot couldn't get the image from his mind, and after the war, he made inquiries to find this monk. He eventually made the journey to San Giovanni Rotondo and recognized the "flying monk" as St. Padre Pio.

TIME TRAVEL AND QUANTUM PHYSICS

The deeper we go in the revelations being imparted to us, the more aware we become that the enemy owns nothing, and God owns everything. The enemy doesn't own the galaxies. He doesn't own the stars. He doesn't own the other planets. There are some Christians who, in their minimalist thinking, try to relegate God's power and His presence, only to the earth. The Lord has created the universes and the galaxies. Science says that there are over 200 galaxies that we know about. I am sure that there is a reason why God created all these things. We can't presume that God might decide someday to cause us to experience trans-relocation or bilocation to one of the galaxies. C. S. Lewis certainly imagined that possibility in his series, *The Space Trilogy,* where Dr. Ranson trans-relocated to Mars and Venus.

I've had experiences where the Lord took me back in time. In one of those experiences, he showed me the explosion in Genesis 1. I saw where God spoke and said, "Let there be light." During that experience, I began to receive a revelation of quantum physics. In 2014, I actually had the opportunity to go to Beijing and speak to the top quantum physicists in all of Asia. It was an astounding experience and seemingly impossible since I barely graduated from high school. That supernatural experience opened the door for me to gain a fuller understanding of quantum physics. I had an experience where God took me into the heavens. I was flying faster than the speed of light, and through that experience, I was able to understand trans-dimensions. I saw that it was a white hole and not a black hole. There was tremendous energy and there was light and sound coming out of another realm that was unseen.

I do believe that people should be open and willing to experience anything God wants to take us through. I think that sometimes our religiosity about certain subjects prevents us from being willing to experience the greater things of the Lord. Why? Because we are afraid of being deceived. The Lord isn't going to bring us into deception; He's going to bring us into a place of fresh revelation.

BILOCATION

Let me state it again: Bilocation is the phenomenon in which a person is in one place at a given time, and at the same moment, by a mysterious miracle, is also in another place. As I would expect, there are those that say this is physically impossible, contrary to all the conditions of matter, as we know them now. However, there have been multiple experiences of bilocation that have been documented. "Bilocation has been mentioned in the lives of numerous saints— their instances of bilocation have been witnessed by trustworthy persons at both of the places where they appeared, even at times being acknowledged by the very saint who performed such a wonder through the grace of God. Additionally, numerous instances of bilocation have been so well-documented, witnessed and investigated that they are accepted facts in the history of the Church."[14]

Whether you know it or not, you are bilocating right now. Paul's words to the church at Ephesus clarify my statement: "...*and raised us up together, and made us sit together in the heavenly places in Christ Jesus.*"[15] This is a perfect place to create a framework for the concept of bilocation.

It would be easy to push this aside and neglect the transcendent experiences of Paul and the apostolic authority in his words, but the theologians join in with an unexpectedly unified position (not all, but many agree).

Meier: "Exaltation into a celestially enlightened, pure and holy, state of life."

Olshausen: "The awakening of the heavenly consciousness."

Expositor's Greek New Testament: "Made us sharers with Him in dignity and dominion, so that even now, and in foretaste of our future exaltation, our life and thought are raised to the heavenlies where He reigns."[16]

Pulpit Commentary: "As God placed Jesus at his right hand in heaven, so he has placed his people with him in heavenly places; i.e. places where the privileges of heaven are dispensed, where the air of heaven is breathed, where the fellowship and the enjoyment of heaven are known, where an elevation of spirit is experienced as if heaven were begun."

SEATED IN HEAVENLY PLACES

You are seated in multiple places right now, in heavenly places. This phrase is translated from the Greek word *epouranios*, meaning "the sphere of spiritual activities."[17] Often, in the book of Ephesians, Paul makes reference to *heavenly places.* It is important to be careful that your religious eye hasn't been trained where you don't see the word *places*, and you see *heaven*, instead of *heavens*. He said heavenly *places*. So, heavenly places are where God rules and reigns. You have been given jurisdiction there. Wherever God rules and reigns as King over His Kingdom has been established, and you are granted a position. You have been given a place to sit in the heavenly places, and this position gives you the jurisdiction and authority to rule with Christ.

> "O Lord, our Lord, how excellent is thy name in all the earth! who hast set thy glory above the heavens. Out of the mouth of babes and sucklings hast thou ordained strength because of thine enemies, that thou mightest still the enemy and the avenger. When I consider thy heavens, the work of thy fingers, the moon and the stars, which thou hast ordained; What is man, that thou art mindful of him? and the son of man, that thou visitest him? For thou hast made him a little lower than the angels, and hast crowned him with glory and honour. Thou madest him to have dominion over the works of thy hands; thou hast put all things under his feet: All sheep and oxen, yea, and the beasts of the field; The fowl of the air, and the fish of the sea, and whatsoever passeth through the paths of the seas. O Lord our Lord, how excellent is thy name in all the earth!"[18]

God has given man dominion over the earth, and through Jesus Christ, we have been given jurisdiction and authority, not just over the earth, but of all creation. That doesn't just include creation on the earth, it includes all creation, the stars, planets, and the unknown regions within the solar system and the universe. In this specific time in human history, there is a massive push for humanity to go to different planets and star systems and, at some point, begin to colonize those places. This is man taking dominion over the universe which God created.[19]

Now, there can be those elements of evil that must be controlled and defeated, but we have to recognize that God is wanting to take the earth and the created universe and bring them into a place of supernatural dominion and authority.

You've been given a seat in the heavenly places. Sit down and take your place! You are a forerunner in the heavenly places. We already have dominion and authority. That's why I believe that the church should be on the forefront of so many issues, and not just taking a backseat and labeling everything as demonic.

There are those that say our location in heavenly places is theological, positional, and spiritual. I take opposition to that statement. I believe that, by possession, we are in heavenly places, not position. God has possessed you and you are a supernatural being that transcends natural humanity, in the sense that you have God living inside of you. The Bible says that the heavens of the heavens cannot contain God, yet your physical body contains God.

"For the earnest expectation of the creation eagerly waits for the revealing of the sons of God."[20]

Creation is not alien to our life and its hopes. It is the natural ally of our souls. What we wish for, creation longs for. Creation is consciously aware of the coming sons of God. With heads erect, outstretched, waiting in suspense, there is a suspicion, a yearning, and a passion for the unveiling revelation of His sons. "What rises from it is the music *of humanity*—not apparently so still and sad to Paul as to Wordsworth, but with a note of hope in its rising triumphantly above all the pain of conflict."[21] The revelation of the sons of God is the result of the entire dominion and transforming supremacy of the Spirit of God in them. They began in conversion and are manifested in glorious transformation. "The Arabic interpreter puts the word *glory* into the text, and reads the word thus, *The earnest expectation of the creature waiteth for the manifestation of the glory of the sons of God;* their glory for the present is hidden, but it shall be discovered and manifested."[22]

It's going to happen whether it's our generation or another generation, because the earnest expectation of all of creation is eagerly waiting for the manifestation of the sons of God. What to do? Take authority!

BILOCATION MYSTICS

Throughout history, there have been unquestionably inexplicable accounts of prophets and priests, preachers and ordinary people who have done just that. Somehow, the laws of our world have been defied when one person is found in two places at the same time. The whole idea seems impossible when considering the rules of physics and matter are unbreakable, yet the accounts of bilocation speak to the contrary.

If the Creator of the laws of nature in our world decides to break those laws, who is to say it cannot be done? Jesus turns water into wine, multiplies the bread and fishes to feed 5000, walks on water, raises Lazarus from the dead, and He Himself walks through a wall. Philip is transported to Azotus, Peter and Paul walk out of a prison, and Paul is trans-relocated to heaven.

Throughout history there are verifiable cases of bilocation. Isidore the Farmer was praying during mass, while plowing in the field.

An elderly man asked St. Joseph of Cupertino if he would kindly assist him at the hour of death. The Saint promised to do so and added, "I shall assist you, even though I should be in Rome." While in Rome, Cupertino was seen talking to the elderly man. Sr. Teresa Fatali asked him how he could be there, since he was still in Rome. Cupertino simply said that he had come to keep his word, and then he disappeared.

St. Lydwine of Schiedam was a victim soul who endured numerous afflictions that kept her perpetually bedridden. The prior of the monastery came to visit her. On one occasion the prior of the monastery of St. Elizabeth, which was hundreds of miles away, came to see her. The Saint gave him a description so detailed of the cells, the chapel, the chapter house, the refectory, and the porters' lodge that the prior was astounded. "But how can you know all this?" he asked in amazement, knowing that she could not leave her bed. "My Father," she replied with a smile, "I have been there frequently when I was in ecstasy."[23]

BOB JONES

I want to share a bilocation story of a man who holds a very special place in my heart, Bob Jones. Bob passed away on February 14, 2014. Bob Jones functioned as a prophet for over forty years. He was influential in three moves of God: IHOP, MorningStar, and Bethel. Bob's first major national exposure was during his time at the prophets' movement in Kansas City. At one point in his life, God promised Bob that he would see the beginning of one billion souls coming into the kingdom in one great wave of the end time harvest. There's a great book on the life of Bob Jones entitled, *Some Said it Thundered*. It is out of print, but you can get used copies on Amazon. The author of the book combines some personal accounts of extraordinary prophecies and some personal encounters in the supernatural.

Bob had several bilocation experiences, where he and even his wife Viola would be bilocated to different places. This is one of my favorite stories. God would send him to different places to minister before he actually even went there on the beginning day of the meetings. He would be sent to minister at a church in a certain nation or even a different part of America. He was scheduled to be there on Friday when the meeting started, but he would be bilocated on a Tuesday or Wednesday. Several of the pastors would say, "Bob, what are you doing here? What are you doing here so early?" And Bob would say, "I just came to have fellowship with you."

Bob would go out to lunch or dinner with these pastors, and while they ate at the restaurant, Bob would be sharing all kinds of information with them, things that were happening in their ministry that needed to be corrected. He would have phenomenal insights to share with them. The ministry was only to the leaders and the pastors since it was private personal input for them. Then, on Friday, Bob would show up. How crazy! The leaders would share their excitement with Bob when he arrived. "Bob, it's been fantastic these last three days. The revelation you've been sharing has totally transformed us." This happened many times and Bob knew that God had bilocated him to those particular places to establish what God was going to do for that weekend. It was as if God wanted to use Bob to minister to them so that there would be greater release and break-through in the region once the meetings started.

I don't believe that he was trying to bilocate. You can't *try* to do these things. In fact, *don't try to do them.* Let God carry you to those places, at His will. Too often, people try to make it happen, when we must let the Lord do it for us!

MARIA OF ÁGREDA, LADY IN BLUE

There is another story I want to share. It is the story of Maria of Ágreda. She was a Spanish nun, abbess (female superior of a commu-nity of nuns), writer, and spiritual director to Philip IV of Spain. She never physically left her village north of Madrid. But, Cecchin, a well-known friar during the 17th century, said he has seen the Spanish records documenting the proof of her bilocation in the Americas. There are many eyewitness accounts to priests and laymen alike describing her "trances," after which she would recall meeting the peoples and missionaries where she went in Texas, Arizona, and New Mexico. Her accounts of the bilocations to the Native Americans began when she was a child. "She says that Jesus inspired her to pray for the Indians of New Spain (Texas, New Mexico, and Arizona) so that their souls would not be lost. The visions of these people and their barbaric customs would become more distinct, and she was urged to pray and sacrifice 'more fervently for these souls.'"[24] In the three years she was reported to have traveled to "New Spain," she appeared at least 500 times to the peoples of Quiviairas, Jumanas, and other areas that are today located in New Mexico, Texas, and Arizona.

There were two particular priests that were sent by the Catholic Church to the Americas to convert the American Indians. When they arrived at the place where they were going to convert the Indians, they immediately began to share the Gospel of Jesus. They discov-ered they had already received the gospel. The gospel came to them through a woman they call the Lady in Blue (the Indians gave her that name because of the color of her order's habit), who flew in the air and came and preached Jesus to them. They told the Indians that this is impossible because the Catholic Church has never sent anyone, much less a woman flying through the air.

She reported several times suffering torture and being left for dead by the Indians who were provoked to violence by their witch doctors. She would come to her senses in her convent with no injuries or marks from the attacks. Then, she would re-appear to the astonished Indians to preach again. Reports of her bilocation were known and investigated while she was alive. She often described to others how she would be "led by angels to unknown countries to preach Jesus Christ" to pagans. In one account, she led 2,000 Indians to be baptized.[25]

That Agreda really and truly visited America many times is attested to in the logs of the Spanish Conquistadors, the French explorers, and the identical accounts by different tribes of Indians a thousand miles apart. Every authentic history of the Southwest of the United States records these mystic phenomena.

BILOCATING INTO THE FUTURE

I had an experience that I wrote about in my book, *Mystical Prayer*. If you don't have the book, I recommend that you buy it. In this experience, I bilocated into the future to a meeting with the dictator of North Korea. I was sitting in my living room and suddenly, boom! I was taken to North Korea, via bilocation. I was in a trancelike experience where I am sitting in my living room and suddenly, I'm in the front of my house. A car pulls up and I get in the car, and inside the car is Kim Jung-un, the North Korean dictator.

I was taken to this meeting of great importance, events that had not happened yet. The Lord revealed to me different things that were going to happen with North Korea. It concerned the United States and the denuclearization of North Korea, and the unification process that would begin between North and South Korea. These events happened during a bilocation experience where God took me into the future.

I know that there are those of you that wonder about the ordeal of bilocating into the future. As I have stated in this book, when I am dealing with a new spiritual encounter or revelation, I always seek to back it up with a Scripture. So, here we go.

"It is he that sitteth upon the circle of the earth, and the inhabitants thereof are as grasshoppers; that stretcheth out the heavens as a curtain, and spreadeth them out as a tent to dwell in."[26]

The word *sitteth* refers to God as a sovereign or monarch, making the circle of the earth His throne. The phrase is designed to show the majesty and glory of God. This word *circle* is important because we understand that a circle is also a cycle. But it's also the angelic throne. God's throne is mobile. Daniel wrote that "His throne was flaming with fire, and its wheels were all ablaze" (Daniel 7:9b NIV). Ezekiel described them as wheels within wheels that rolled in any direction.

If you have my teaching on angels in the School of Angels, you will hear me talk about how God doesn't sit on animate objects; He rides in angelic structures. And that structure is circular in motion. It's a wheel within a wheel. It's a throne. The circle here is actually translated to mean the vault of the heavens, or the circuit, or the compass which arches over the earth.

There is a place where God rests above, and this is the eternal realm. The chronological time moves from points in history to the next, moving from one point to the next successive point. This is chronological time. Chronological time is here, and it moves from one successive moment to the next. That's how it works. However, God does not live in this realm, nor does He live underneath it. Man has not been called to live underneath time; man has been called to live above time. If you are a new creation in Christ, you have actually been called to live in heavenly places, which includes outside of time and space. This is the time frame of the eternal realm.

So, today is here and tomorrow is here. You are bilocating at two places already, as you are seated with Him in heavenly places. You are seated with Him in the circle above the earth, and the inhabitants of the earth are as grasshoppers. Who are those inhabitants? Those are the people that are not saved and that are not sitting in heavenly places. They are the grasshoppers of humanity. It is always our prayer that they will be converted and join us in the heavenly places.

Isaiah says that He stretches out the heavens like a curtain and spreads them out as a tent. "Perhaps the idea is that the heavens are extended like a tent, in order to furnish a dwelling-place for God and His children. Thus, the Chaldee renders it. If so, it proves that the universe, so vast, was suited to be the dwelling place of the High and Holy One and is a most impressive representation of His immensity."[27]

He stretches out the heavens and spreads them like a tent, as a dwelling place. So, if you are seated somewhere, you are dwelling there. You are dwelling under the stretched-out tent that has room for everyone. The dwelling place is *the abiding place*. The word *dwell* means *to abide, sit, and remain*.

Curtain, veil, and dwelling place. Communion be for all. But there is only one way. It is through the veil to the communion place, and that is by the blood of the Lamb. Drink of His blood and eat of His flesh and be renewed and cleansed in the heavenly places. You are no longer striving to enter into eternity. You have found rest outside of time and space as you partake of Communion. You are in Isaiah 40:22. You are in Ephesians 2:6. You are entering into Romans 8:19. You are living and dwelling in that place, through the flesh, through the veil, and through the curtain of time. You are seated in the heavenly places, with Christ.

"Beyond the veil is where I witness all Your glory
Seated on Your throne in majesty and power
I lay prostrate before You, oh my King
In this place of sweet communion;
This is my earnest prayer
This is my earnest plea
And You'll bid me
You'll say come ye beyond the veil"[28]

7 / GENETICAL TRANSFIGURATIONS, PART ONE

IT IS MY DESIRE TO ASSIST YOU IN THE JOURNEY GOD HAS DESTINED FOR you. It's not really a destination, but more like a mysterious journey into the miraculous. The things I will share in this chapter could be considered exotic theology. I title it *exotic* because it will require a deep dive into the Scriptures to find the material I will share. This isn't just inconsequential, superficial Christianity that we are looking for. We are looking for a demonstration of God's power both in Word and in Spirit. This theological adventure will be sort of an exotic distraction from simple, straightforward Bible study you would experience in a typical church. I promise you, this will not be boring, nor typical.

"*I will praise You, for I am fearfully and wonderfully made; Marvelous are Your works, And that my soul knows very well.*"[1] God's ceaseless wisdom and imposing power, exhibited in the staggering and intriguing composition of the human body, and infused with astonishing wonder, should lead us to the place of worship of our great God.

One poses themselves in contemplation of the phenomenon of the human body, the beauty of the mind, the complexity of DNA and genetic codes, the creative texture of the human skin, the exact composure and perfect proportions of all its parts. Virtuous is every bone, muscle, artery, nerve, and fiber. They are perfectly framed and placed to answer their designed end. Those who apprehend and appreciate the creative work of God stand in awe of the mind of the Maker.

I believe God gives us the opportunity to respect and investigate the complexities of His creation. Francis Collins, a medical doctor, is director of the National Human Genome Research Institute and is passionate about science. But the self-described Bible-believing Christian is just as passionate about his faith (which he came to after reading C.S. Lewis) as he is about his work.

"Collins sees the chance to uncover the incredible intricacies of God's creation as an occasion of worship. To be able to look, for the first time in human history, at all three billion letters of the human DNA—which I think of as God's language—gives us just a tiny glimpse into the amazing creative power of his mind. Every discovery that we now make in science [is], for me, a chance to worship him in a broader sense, to appreciate just in a small bit the amazing grandeur of his creation."[2]

INVESTIGATING THE TRUTH

Before we begin the exploration of Genetic Transfiguration, I am wondering how many of you that read this book will be hungry enough to go into the depths of what God wants to reveal. The deeper you go, the more controversial, but it will be astounding. There is a principal I embrace that is critical to learning. It is a principle proclaimed by Albert Einstein: "Condemnation that comes before investigation is the highest form of ignorance." Too often, when we are presented a new idea or truth, we don't take the time to investigate. We quickly move straight to condemnation, probably because of laziness. When I hear people talk about closed heavens over territories, I find that the majority of closed heavens are between people's ears. God will never violate His Word, but it has been known that He often violates our understanding of it, to bring us into a deeper understanding of His mind.

That's enough, it is time for a deep dive.

"Even so, the thoughts of God no one knows except the Spirit of God. Now we have received, not the spirit of the world, but the Spirit who is from God, so that we may know the things freely given to us by God, which things we also speak, not in words taught by human wisdom, but in those taught by the Spirit, combining spiritual thoughts with spiritual words."[3]

Are you extracting from Paul's words the weight of His revelation concerning the thoughts of God and the position of the Holy Spirit to reveal spiritual truth to His people? If you don't understand this truth, you will be left in the dark, because we cannot understand these truths without a little divine assistance. No one knows the thoughts of God. The Holy Spirit, the Alongside One, reveals to us the things that God wants to give to us. God's thoughts are made available to us through the Holy Spirit. The Holy Spirit reveals spiritual thoughts to your mind and then those thoughts are transformed into spiritual words that can be communicated to others.

ONE BECAME MANY

I love this quote by Polycarp, who was a disciple of John the Revelator: "Therefore forsaking the vanity of many and their false doctrines let us return to the world which has been handed down to us from the beginning."[4] I believe that there is a plumb line of revelation that's coming to the body of Christ. I sense that it will take us into an apostolic understanding of the kingdom of God. I sense that the Western Church has been settling for something less than God's best, but I believe that will change.

Saint Irenaeus was a disciple of Polycarp and was a great teacher during the 2nd and 3rd generation church. He codified as Scripture not only the Old Testament but most of the books now known as the New Testament, His work included the exclusion of many works, including a large number of the Gnostic works that flourished in the

2nd century.[5] This is such a persuasive quote by Irenaeus: "The only true and steadfast Teacher, the Word of God, our Lord Jesus Christ, through His transcendent love, became what we are, that He might bring us to be what He is Himself."[6]

> "And the Word was made flesh, and dwelt among us, (and we beheld his glory, the glory as of the only begotten of the Father,) full of grace and truth."[7]

> "To whom God would make known what is the riches of the glory of this mystery among the Gentiles; which is Christ in you, the hope of glory:"[8]

> "In Christ Jesus you are all sons of God, through faith."[9]

In the incarnation, Jesus Christ becomes flesh and the glory was that Christ put on an earthly garb and lived (tabernacled) among us. Man came to be a son of God, because the Son of God became a man. The infinite and finite become as one. "The Logos, which was in the beginning, has now become; the Logos which was God became flesh; the Logos that was with God has set up his tabernacle among us." [10]

He became flesh and lived among us so that when He submitted Himself to the torture of the Cross, we might become His sons and daughters. Christ is in you and you are in Christ. He has transcended and multiplied Himself into all of us, and together, we become the body of Christ. This is Orthodox Christianity. This is the truth of the Word of God, that God would come and live on the inside of us and manifest Himself through us.

Saint Irenaeus wrote these gripping words: "The glory of God is a human being fully alive and being alive consists in beholding God." For this reason, God, who cannot be clutched, comprehended, or seen, permits Himself to be seen, comprehended, and clutched by men, that He may give life to those who see and receive Him. "It is impossible to live without life, and the actualization of life comes from participation in God, while participation in God is to see God and enjoy His goodness. If the revelation of God through creation gives life to all who live upon the earth, much more does the manifestation of the Father through the Word give life to those who see God."[11]

DNA OF GOD

"But we all, with open face beholding as in a glass the glory of the Lord, are <u>*changed into the same image*</u> *from glory to glory, even as by the Spirit of the Lord."*[12] *"For whom he did foreknow, he also did predestinate to be* <u>*conformed to the image of his Son."*</u>[13] The intent of these two verses are clear: Christians have received the reflected glory of the Divine nature and presence, as Moses received it on his countenance. The mirrored glory is metamorphosed into the same image, the image of Christ.[14] The believer is fashioned and formed into the image of Christ. We "faintly give back what we adore," and man, in his measure and degree, becomes, as he was meant to be at his creation, like Christ, "the image of the invisible God."[15]

BATTLE OF THE SEEDS

I know that Satan hates the message of sonship and the blood and the DNA of God. It was that satanic system that he created through the fall of man and that was released through Cain when he slew his brother. The blood of the innocent being poured into the earth that actually laid the foundation for the first human city.

As you study the Scriptures, you will find that neither Adam nor Seth sought to construct the first human earth-bound city. It was Cain that built the first city. *"And Cain went out from the presence of the Lord, and dwelt in the land of Nod, on the east of Eden. And Cain knew his wife; and she conceived, and bare Enoch: and he builded a city, and called the name of the city, after the name of his son, Enoch."*[16] "The story of Cain includes rejected worship, murder of his brother, and a sentence to be a wanderer on earth until he built his city. The God of the Bible wants us to consider the deeper lessons of this narrative. The real story of human development is the contrast and strivings of two cities, the doomed city of man and the ultimately triumphant 'city of God.'"[17] God will eventually accomplish His purpose through Abraham.

> "Now the LORD had said to Abram: "Get out of your country, From your family and from your father's house, To a land that I will show you."[18]

> "For he looked for a city which hath foundations, whose builder and maker is God."[19]

God makes His choice in contrast to Cain and his choices. Abraham is God's choice, for he was perfect in God's sight. Abraham will leave the city and head toward Canaan. Abraham would find a city whose architect and builder is God. But the war will always be there, the war between good and evil.

There has always been a war, a war of the seeds. Do you remember God's words to the serpent? He said, *"I'm going to put enmity between your seed and her seed. You're going to bruise his heel, but he's going to crush your head."*[20] When Adam took of that forbidden fruit, he fell multiple layers through many, many dimensions. He was thrust into a matrix where he could only see the three dimensions, while God has 12 dimensions.

THE BLUEPRINT

The original human being had uncorrupted DNA actively working and maintaining the full function of the human as a spiritual being. As a result of the fall of Adam, the heart centers of the DNA strands closed down. As the consequence of this loss, we are living in a spiritually deficient society where intuitive and spiritual abilities have been greatly reduced. I have a prime conjecture that I will present in this chapter. It will definitely stretch your thinking. Before I present my concepts, I will need to submit biological information on DNA, which I will build upon and do some repetition as we move forward in this chapter.

DNA has four main building blocks. "We call these nitrogenous bases: Adenine (A), Thymine (T), Guanine (G), and Cytosine (C). If you think of the structure of DNA as a ladder, the rungs of the ladder (where you would put your hands) are made from the nitrogenous bases. These bases pair up to make each step of the ladder. The most common DNA shape illustrated by artists and scientists looks a lot like a twisting ladder. Scientists call this a double helix. DNA does more than store information. It is also able to make copies of itself. To do this, it first has to unzip the nitrogenous bases. All the pairs of 'AT' and 'GC' are separated. The DNA then has two single strands."[21]

The discovery of the DNA double helix is a hallowed story of scientific triumph. "The work of four researchers merging together to solve one of science's biggest mysteries, giving birth to what we know as the field of modern genetics. But decades later, we're still learning that DNA is a more furiously complicated piece of biological machinery than we ever knew."[22] The DNA is the human blueprint. It's made up of the nucleic acids and a system of extremely complex molecules filled with the information that creates the physical existence. Our DNA is therefore our personal blueprint, and as such, it contains our physical, mental, and spiritual information.

The Logos Word is a living spirit, not just a bound book. Heraclitus, a Greek philosopher, first used the term Logos around 600 B.C. to designate the divine reason, or plan, which coordinates a changing universe. This word was well suited for John's purpose in John 1. In the Greek Lexicon, the author translated John 1 with this creative use of language. John creates a declaration of poetic beauty. "The essential Word of God, Jesus Christ, the personal wisdom and power in union with God, his minister in creation and government of the universe, the cause of all the world's life both physical and ethical, which for the procurement of man's salvation put on human nature in the person of Jesus."[23]

The essence of the word *logos* means *blueprint.* The divine blueprint is contained in the mind of God. Within the Logos is the very life and the mind of God. The more you enter into and discover the mind of God, the more you begin to understand the depths of revelation that are possible. God's mental powers are so incalculably superior to ours. Wouldn't it be somewhat like a six-year-old trying to understand the people who built a rocket to take humans to the moon?

"For who hath known the mind of the Lord, that he may instruct him? but we have the mind of Christ."[24] In this verse, Paul uses an imperfect syllogistic argument. The question: Who has known the mind of Christ? The response: But we have the mind of Christ. The argument is settled in this matter. The natural man cannot comprehend the Lord's plans, His intentions, His feelings, His views, and His designs. However, the spiritual man is taught by the Holy Spirit, who has the mind of Christ, who has the mind of God. It is for this reason that Paul emphasizes the importance of renewing the mind, the spirit of the mind.

DNA AND THE CREATION STORY

"And God said, 'Let us make man in our image, after our likeness.'"[25] I won't spend time reviewing the trinitarian language in this verse, but what I am interested in are these words, "Let us make man in our image." Made in His image, made in His likeness. There is a certain distinction of the human body that relates upward to God. However, it is in the spirit and soul that the real image/likeness are reflected. "Like God, man's soul and *spirit,* immaterial, invisible, active, intelligent, free, immortal, and, when first created, endowed with a high degree of divine knowledge, and with holiness and righteousness; He was also invested with an image of God's authority and dominion, and was constituted the ruler, under Him, of all the inferior creatures."[26]

When you begin to understand that your DNA shifts, you see that your physical body can, as well. The human genome takes shape and shifts over time. DNA twists and turns into interacting sections that determine what a cell does and when. DNA holds the genetic codes within everything, from every living organism, like a blade of grass, to someone's eyeball. The way that the codes are laid out determine the manifestation of things in the natural. The DNA that determines the color of your eye is the same DNA that makes up your heart. The Codon factor is the genetic coding that determines the DNA formation.

The Book of Beginnings, the Book of Genesis, holds the mysteries and the foundations of our world. Thus, we are called to unravel the mysteries of God's intentions in the creation of the world, especially those early verses of chapter one. God told Adam to replenish the earth, but before that command, we read that the earth was without form and void. God never creates anything incomplete, so there was something that took place between Genesis 1:1 and Genesis 1:2. "*And the earth was without form, and void; and darkness was upon the face of the deep. And the Spirit of God moved upon the face of the waters.*" The literal Hebrew for *was* is actually the word *became*. So, the reading would be that the earth became without form... There is much debate on what caused this disruption in the creation process.

The interesting part is that the whole earth was covered with water. It was like the earth was in a womb, like an unborn baby is in the womb of a mother. Then the Bible says that the Spirit hovered over the deep, over the waters. In the process, there was a vibration. The "Law of Vibration," states that everything in existence, both seen and unseen, when taken to its most basic form, consists of pure energy, and exists as a vibratory pattern.[27]

The Spirit was brooding over the waters. He was waiting for the time when God's mind would begin to manifest in creative wonder. Because He said that in His mind, you were there. Before you were ever here, you are already there. You are already in His mind and in His thoughts.

THE TWO ADAMS

"*All who dwell on the earth will worship him, whose names have not been written in the Book of Life of the Lamb slain from the foundation of the world.*"[28] The whole universe is founded upon the blood of Jesus Christ. He is the lamb that was slain from the foundation of the world. Laying upon the earth was the blood of Christ, or the genetic code of God. The former, in the Greek, is more obvious. "Whatsoever virtue was in the sacrifices, did operate through Messiah's death alone. As He was *the Lamb slain from the foundation of the world*, so all atonements ever made were only effectual by His blood" (Bishop Pearson, Exposition of the Creed).[29] The blood of Jesus was poured out for us before the creation of the world, but was only revealed to us when Jesus was crucified on the Cross.

"And the Lord God formed man out of the dust of the ground."[30] There is going to be a generation that's going to move both in the Word and the Spirit. They can try to deny revelation, but when it's founded on the Word of God, then there can be no more argument. That's why God wants us to be a mystical people and people of His Word. The last day's move of God is going to be a move of the Word and of the Spirit. The Word of God is going to be our foundation, our springboard to take us into greater depths of revelation.

You are the only thing in creation that God physically implanted His blueprint. The specialists say that every human being has a unique fingerprint and they can tell who you are by your print. That is incredible. Your identity can even be determined by a simple fingerprint. But when God made you, He formed you with His fingerprint, or His blueprint, or His DNA. The Bible says that Adam was formed out of the dust of the ground. Laying on the dust of the ground was the very blood of His Son, blood that was slain from the foundation of the world. Peter makes it clear, in 1 Peter 1:18-19, that we are "redeemed from the empty way of life by the blood of Christ" and that this was accomplished "before the creation of the world."

Back to Genesis 2:7, where it is said that man (*adam*) was formed from the dust of the ground. This stage of the creation is very different from the other phases. Adam is shaped and formed from dust, while in the other creative processes they were created out of nothing. "As regards man's body, Jehovah forms it from the dust of the ground, the *adâmâh*, or fruitful arable soil, so called from Adam, for whose use it was specially fitted, and by whom it was first tilled. But the main intention of the words is to point out man's feebleness. He is made, not from the rocks, nor from ores of metal, but from the light, shifting particles of the surface, blown about by every wind."[31] Yet, frail as is man's body, God breathes into his nostrils the breath of life and he lives.

Adâmâh is closely connected to Adam. In a sense, man was formed by God and created in an earth suit so that he would forever be connected to the earth. When Adam fell, he caused humanity to fall with him; all of creation fell under the curse. The whole universe came into a planetary distortion. Outside of time and space, resting above the chaos, the lamb of God was slain. God had the solution before there was a problem. God formed the man before the 'tick tock' of time. He placed him in Eden and then He formed him with an eternal code on the inside of him. If man would have been in time, he would have been subjected to time. Man was created outside of time so that He could hold him within the DNA that contains the eternal and not the temporal. Therefore, by this eternal clock, man could be saved.

For years, science has recognized that we have two active physical strands of DNA. It is called the double helix. By revelation, we begin to understand that the fall of man was not final. Within our DNA is the government of God, His fullness that needs to be activated in the new creation. The only way that a man can activate the fullness of his DNA is through the rebirth. Lying dormant within the DNA is all of earth's distortions caused by the fall of humankind. As a result of Adam's fall, he created a planetary DNA twisted alteration that has caused every living organism's DNA to falsely appear as a base with only four chemicals: A, T, C, G. That's how the DNA is aligned, which made man susceptible to mutations and manipulations of his genetic code, allowing distorted DNA to manifest in his fallen genetic code.

Mankind was locked into the eternal prison of sin and shame, arrogance and anger, and delusions and deceptions. God's plan would not be thwarted; it would be fulfilled. He would send His Son into the chambers of time, where He would be able to set His people free. When Adam fell, time never knew that Christ had died. Time was waiting for a future moment, the moment of restoration. *"Whom heaven must receive until the times of restoration of all things, which God has spoken by the mouth of all His holy prophets since the world began."*[32]

We long for a restoration, which is greater than a restitution. There's a difference between restoration and restitution. Restoration is if someone loans you $5 and many years later, they come to you and they give you $5. They say, "I owe you this debt of $5." But restitution involves compound interest laid upon it. When somebody comes back and they say, "I owe you $5," then you say to them, "Well, there was interest upon that. There is compound interest and you owe me more than $5, now you owe me all the interest on top of that." Shocked, he will ask, "What are you talking about Charlie?" "You know what, I'm going to put a timing mechanism on this thing. I want more than the restoration. I want to have restitution. I want there to be compound interest, so that when My Son comes to the earth and dies, He won't just replace the first Adam, He will be the Son of God. There will be a second Adam that has the capability to move in greater dimensions than even the first Adam."

"And so, it is written, the first man Adam was made a living soul; the last Adam was made a quickening spirit." Howbeit that was not first which is spiritual, but that which is natural; and afterward that which is spiritual. The first man is of the earth, earthy; the second man is the Lord from heaven. As is the earthy, such are they also that are earthy: and as is the heavenly, such are they also that are heavenly. And as we have borne the image of the earth, we shall also bear the image of the heavenly.[33] Paul was not speaking rhetorically, but prophetically. Tertullian says, "Let us bear; not we shall bear, perceptively (by instruction), not permissive (by promise)."[34]

The first Adam was created perfect from the dust of the ground. His disobedience brought sin into the world. Jesus is *the second, and the last Adam*. He was the last man who did not have a sin nature. By virtue of His sinless nature, Jesus was able to be the sinless sacrifice for the sins of the world.

Everything that the enemy has stolen from man will not just be restored; there will be restitution and that will be with compound interest. Those that are redeemed by the blood of the Lamb are restored and receive restitution. Satan had one desire: to cause man to disobey and then to fall. He wanted the DNA within man so that he could have the earth to himself. That's why you study Ezekiel 28 and Isaiah 14, so you discover Satan was actually given the earth but, in his fall, it was taken from him. *"How you have fallen from heaven, O star of the morning, son of the dawn! You have been cut down to the earth, you who have weakened the nations! I will ascend above the heights of the clouds; I will make myself like the Most High."*[35] God hovered over the earth, the earth that was in chaos and disarray, because of Satan's pride that caused his great fall from heaven to the earth. I have a sense that the words God spoke to Satan went something like this: "Satan, the thing that you wanted so desperately, I'm going to lay within man, the very genetic code that will give him dominion and power over all of the earth."

THE HEREDITARY CODE

As I have said, God formed man outside of time so that his genetic code would have time for a restoration and restitution. We also understand that Eve was taken out of the side of Adam. Bone of my bone, flesh of my flesh. Adam was the original blueprint. He had the genetic code that was inside of him in creation. The Bible says that the heaven of the heavens cannot contain God.[36] *"Or do you not know that your body is the temple of the Holy Spirit who is in you, whom you have from God, and you are not your own? For you were bought at a price; therefore glorify God in your body and in your spirit, which are God's."*[37] So, the heaven of the heavens cannot contain God, but your physical body can. The universe with all its wonder is marvelous, but the human body is more amazing, since it can contain God.

There had to be a second Adam that would come and redeem all of creation. In the natural birth, you have two bloodlines, one from your mother and one from your father. You have been given either an X, or a Y chromosome, depending upon whether you're a male or a female, that comes from your father. The X chromosome was provided by your mother, but the Y or the X, the Y, if you're a male, the X, if you're a female, was provided by your father. Within that Y or X is the distortions of all human history. The genetic code lies dormant because of the fall of man allowing the satanic manipulations that took place when Adam also ate of the fruit. That's why many demonic things lie dormant within the DNA of man. Within the bloodline of man is iniquity from the fall and as a result that iniquity changed the DNA structure resulting in those genetic changes that have been passed down from one generation to the next. As you study the word of God you will discover that there was no offering for iniquity under the Old Testament law. The Bible clearly indicates that *iniquity* is in relation to man's heart and has a distinct relationship to mans spirit as well.

"Blessed is the man unto whom the LORD imputeth not iniquity, and in whose spirit there is no guile." (Psalms 32:2)

If sin is the fruit of the fall then iniquity is the seed from which it grows. Iniquity is the sum total of all twisted and manipulated darkness within mankind. It is there with human beings at conception and a spiritual inheritance of sin is passed down. It is a spiritual cord which transmits DNA of evil from one generation to another. Iniquity permeates man's heart. It is a force compelling good people to commit sin. It fills us with unbelief, causes sickness, addictions and greed to manifest in the human heart. It is our spiritual DNA that stores all of this information. There was only one cure from this curse and His name was Jesus Christ. The blood of the only begotten Son of God is the only thing that can wipe away generations upon generations of darkness held within our DNA.

Consider these words written by Peter. "*According to his divine power, he has given unto us. According to his divine power, not our power. He has given unto us all things pertaining unto life and godliness through the knowledge of him that has called us unto glory and virtue, whereby we are given us exceeding great and precious promises that by these we might become, might be partakers of the divine nature.*"[38] Peter puts great stress on preachers and theologians; a stress that forces one to interpret by way of exegesis, instead of eisegesis. *Eisegesis* means reading your bias into the Scriptures while *exegesis* means to let the Scripture *read you* without previous prejudice. It has been my desire to interpret correctly to the best of my ability without losing the revelation I have received. To my conservative, anti-supernatural theologians, I pray that you will be able to leave your biblical bias at the table and seek to interpret according to your gifts and, maybe more importantly, by the Holy Spirit.

With that in mind, let's proceed. "The human is kindred with the divine. The drop of water is of one nature with the boundless ocean that rolls shoreless beyond the horizon and stretches plumbless into the abysses. The tiniest spark of flame is of the same nature as those leaping, hydrogen spears of illuminated gas that spring hundreds of thousands of miles high in a second or two in the great central sun. The Christian man lives only by continual derivation of life from God; and forever and ever the secret of his being and of his blessedness is not that he has become a possessor, but that he has become a partaker of the Divine nature."[39]

Having escaped the corruption that is in the world through lust, there is a promise that God gave through His Son that has been transferred inwardly to us through Jesus Christ dying on the Cross. A divine power, a divine nature comes to us from the Most High God. There is a second birth, a rebirth, a reforming of your DNA that activates the spiritual aspects that were dormant.

When Jesus hung on the Cross and His side was pierced, the Bible says that out of His side poured blood and water that fell to the earth. Redeeming the earth, redeeming man, so that whosoever would call upon the name of the Lord would be saved. Saved from what? The corruption that is in the world through lust. Through the blood of Christ, our DNA is shifted, renewed, and we create an alignment within ourselves allowing us to shift into a much higher vibrational level and frequency of light. The spiritual man has been awakened to a new reality, a reality of the divine nature that is now part of us.

PARTICIPATING IN THE DIVINE NATURE

In Scripture, we can trace a line from Peter to Irenaeus, St. Athanasius, and Maximos the Confessor. In 2 Peter 1:4, which I have already quoted, we start the chain. *"Through these he has given us his very great and precious promises, so that through them you may <u>participate in the divine nature</u>."* Now we move on to voices in the 1st and 2nd centuries.

St. Maximos the Confessor (580-662): "A sure warrant for looking forward with hope to deification of human nature is provided by the incarnation of God, which makes man god to the same degree as God himself became man... For it is clear that He who became man without sin (cf. Heb. 4:15) will divinize human nature without changing it into the divine nature, and will raise it up for his own sake to the same degree as He lowered Himself for man's sake" (*Philokalia*, Vol. II, 178).

St. Irenaeus in the 2nd century, who wrote of "the Word of God, our Lord Jesus Christ, who did, through His transcendent love, become <u>what we are</u>, that He might bring us to be even <u>what He is Himself</u>" (*Against Heresies*, Book V, preface).

St. Athanasius wrote, "God became man so that man might become god" (*On the Incarnation* 54:3).

The Bible is full of references to the "in Christ" union. It is a theme that Paul used in his writings to the churches that he addressed in his letters. Peter used the phrase "participating in the divine nature." It is not outside of biblical interpretation to declare that we have participated **in divine nature. We once participated in Adam and all humanity was impacted by his fall.** In Christ, we participate in a new head of humanity, Christ the Messiah.

"In Christ, the two natures of God and human are not two persons but one; thus, a union is effected in Christ, between all of humanity and God. So, the Holy God and sinful humanity are reconciled in principle, in the one sinless man, Jesus Christ."[40] The prayer of Jesus in John 17 convincingly illustrates the oneness of God and man. *"I do not pray for these alone, but also for those who will believe in Me through their word; that they all may be one, as You, Father, are in Me, and I in You;*

that they also may be one in Us, that the world may believe that You sent Me."[41]

Thomas Aquinas taught that "full participation in divinity" is humankind's true beatitude and the destiny of human life (*Summa Theology* 3.1.2).

Cyril of Alexandria commented that we are all called to take part in divinity, becoming the likeness of Christ and the image of the Father by "participation."[42]

In the Orthodox Church, the concept of experiencing the divine nature of God is neither new nor startling. The theological phrase for this concept is *theosis*. Theosis is the understanding that human beings can have real union with God, and so become like God to such a degree that we participate in the divine nature.

I love the personal feel of how Frederica Mathewes-Green interprets theosis. It is a process, a soaking in the presence of God that not only fills our spirits but our bodies also. God expects us to grow and change till we become <u>crammed with God's presence</u>. Green uses Moses and the burning bush as an example of *theosis*. The bush was on fire but not being consumed, bearing the supernatural light. "God comes in our hearts and in the center of our being and illuminates us and shines his light in us and through us."[43]

This brings to mind Philippians 2:12–13, where St. Paul tells us to "work out [our] salvation with fear and trembling," for it is God who is at work in us both to will and to do for His good pleasure. Thus, we get a clear picture here of the process by which "we are renewed and unified so completely with God that we become by grace what God is by nature. God works in us, and we cooperate with His grace."[44]

In order to dig a little deeper, it would be helpful to examine the biblical word 'work', which is actually a misuse of the Greek word, which is *energeo*, which means energy. Theologians made a distinct and erroneous decision, choosing to use the Latin word 'work' for the Greek word *energeo*. The more accurate translation would be energizing. In Philippians 2:13, Precept Austin interprets the verse with these words: "*it is God Who is all the while effectually at work in you [energizing and creating in you the power and desire], both...in us (present tense*

= *Again emphasizing the continual **energizing** effect of the Holy Spirit.*)[45] Doesn't that make these Scriptures enthuse you in a great way?"

Orthodox theologians have been careful to distinguish between God's essence and His energies. God is incomprehensible in His essence. But God, who is love, allows us to know Him through His divine energies. It is through these divine energies and the resulting actions whereby He reveals Himself to us in creation, providence, and redemption. It is through the divine energies, therefore, that we achieve union with God.

The theology of the Eastern Church distinguishes the nature (or essence) and the energies as declared by the well-known Orthodox theologian Vladimir Lossky, who was influenced by St. Gregory Palamas.

"The doctrine of the energies, ineffably distinct from the essence, is the dogmatic basis of the real character of all mystical experience. God, who is inaccessible in His essence, is present in His energies 'as in a mirror,' remaining invisible in that which He is; 'in the same way we are able to see our faces, themselves invisible to us in a glass,' according to a saying of St. Gregory Palamas. (Sermon on the Presentation of the Holy Virgin in the Temple). Wholly unknowable in His essence, God wholly reveals Himself in His energies, which yet in no way divide His nature into two parts–knowable and unknowable–but signify two different modes of the divine existence, in the essence and outside of the essence."[46]

THE PERFECT GENETIC CODE

The DNA that has been placed in our new creation is beginning to be activated, so that we move outside of human existence and become a supernatural being on the earth, who lives and moves and has their being in Christ. Generically, each person is participating in the divine nature. The reason why is because collectively, as humans, we are God's offspring and thus share in His nature. In Acts 17:28, we are confronted with a compelling truth. *"For in Him we live and move and have our being, as also some of your own poets have said, 'For we are also*

His offspring." Meyers NT offers their comments on this verse: "Man is in such intimate connection with God, that he is constantly surrounded by the Godhead and embraced in its essential influence, but, apart from the Godhead, could neither live, nor move, nor exist."[47]

Biblical Hermeneutics Stack Exchange is a question and answer site exclusively for theologians and professors. They had a fascinating conversation about generic participation. "Generically, each person is participating in the divine nature. The reason why is because collectively as humans we are God's offspring and thus, share in his nature. The biological metaphor serves to explain our relationship with God in our natural state."[48]

The conversation continued with this presentation: "In Genesis, we read that God created man in his own image and likeness. It is written that God made the body alive by giving it a spirit. The living soul is therefore what the image of God refers to. This simply means that human existence is a visible picture of the invisible God. When man speaks, reasons and creates, he shows what God is like.[49]

Romans 8:16, 17 says, *"that the Spirit itself bears witness with our spirit. That we are children of God and if children, then heirs, and heirs of God and joint heirs with Christ."* When Jesus was born through Mary, the Bible says that the angel Gabriel came to Mary, and said, "You are perfect in God's sight." What was he talking about? He was saying that you have a perfect genetic code within you, a code that had not been distorted.

The Holy Spirit came and overshadowed the woman just like He overshadowed the earth. The purpose of this overshadowing was to watch over the blood of man, so that a Savior could be born with an uncorrupted bloodline. "I'm going to put an enmity between your seed and My seed." This was an automatic war that began between the seeds.

Over the years, men have sought to destroy bloodlines. God looked for a woman to give birth to His Son that had a perfect blood line and genetic code. Joseph and Mary had been visited by an angel and told that Herod would attempt to kill Jesus, their Son. The Magi arrive in Jerusalem seeking for the King; they had been told Messiah was born. The Magi arrive in Herod's court with these words that would arouse his anger. *"Where is the One who has been born King of the Jews? We saw His star when it rose and have come to worship Him."* Herod was furious and knew that there was a potential king in the royal bloodline. Herod had planned to make the Magi tell him of the whereabouts of the Christ child. When he heard of the Magi's change in course, he grew angry. Herod would take no chances. The bloodline must be cut off. He tried to kill the infant Messiah by killing all the young children in the area, an event known as the Massacre of the Innocents.

After the fall, everything on the earth had been corrupted, even animals had been corrupted. Everything had fallen. The *Book of Jasher*, mentioned in the biblical books of Joshua and Second Chronicles, was faithfully translated into English from the Rabbinical Hebrew in approximately A.D. 1840. It is quoted in Joshua 10:13 and 2 Samuel 2:18. The translator correctly points out that although it is not divine Scripture, it nevertheless is a mighty historical and ancient work which relates directly to biblical historical times and events. You see that when Cain was killed, he was actually mistaken for an animal. Something took place within Cain, a genetic mutation that caused even the human beings on the earth at that time to know Cain. They saw him in a field, and he was not human. *"And Tubal Cain told his father to draw his bow, and with the arrows he smote Cain, who was yet far off, and he slew him, for he appeared to them to be an animal."*[50] You can see these incidents throughout human history, even with Nebuchadnezzar, when he lost his mind. The Bible says that his fingernails grew out like an animal on him. This was more than a psychological breakdown.

God breathed into man the breath of life and made him a living soul. Your soul is what connects you both in the realm of the spirit and to your physical body. That's why your soul can move in between those two realms. But God said, all men have become corrupt. *"So, God looked upon the earth, and indeed it was corrupt; for all flesh had corrupted their way on the earth."*

God felt sorry for mankind. I believe that God would look for a perfect genetic code, one that has not been corrupted.

It went from Mary's earth DNA, and when it switched over, it didn't go to a natural Adam or the fallen man. It went right into Jesus. This is what makes Jesus Christ so amazing, so loved. Because when His DNA switched over, it was the blood of God running through His veins.

Mary played her part, and it was a miraculous part she played. It must be stated that the intricate details of how God worked within the body of Mary are not given to us. All that is revealed is that the virgin birth was a supernatural act of God.

"Mary said to the angel, 'How can this be, since I do not know a man?' And the angel answered and said to her, 'The Holy Spirit will come upon you, and the power of the Highest will overshadow you; therefore, also, that Holy One who is to be born will be called the Son of God.'"[51] What was in her, was of her and of God. The woman tied Christ to the earth.

Adam, the first man, was a new creation in the earth of a garden. The birth of Jesus is beyond the miracle of Adam's birth. The Bible presents Adam as the *first Adam* and gives the Lord Jesus Christ the curious title of the *last Adam*. God breathed into Adam's nostrils the breath of life, and he became a living soul. Jesus descended from heaven and was given birth by a virgin. The last Adam, Jesus, was victorious over sin, the flesh, and the devil.

Adam was created by God. The second Adam was God. Jesus did what Adam could have never done. Christ walked on the earth, manifesting the glory, living in an earthly garment, but with a perfect genetic code.

THE MAN CHRIST JESUS

One of the heresies that has been debated for centuries is that *Jesus Christ was not a human being.* That is a heresy. Jesus Christ was a human. He was fully God and fully man. Two natures in one person. The most widely accepted definitions of the incarnation and the nature of Jesus were made by the First Council of Nicaea in 325, the

Council of Ephesus in 431, and the Council of Chalcedon in 451. The Athanasian Creed recognized this doctrine and affirmed its importance, stating that "He is God from the essence of the Father, begotten before time; and he is human from the essence of his mother, born in time. Incarnation is vital for understanding the concept of divinization of the Man, most well and elaborately developed in Orthodox Christianity and most well expressed by Church Fathers, such as St. Athanasius of Alexander and St Cyril of Alexandria."[52]

There are those that say that Jesus was able to perform the miracles because He was God. If you were not God, you would perform no miracles. Some say that He went to the Cross as a spirit being, not as a man. Donatism was developed in the 3rd century and it was a doctrine that "the phenomenon of Jesus, his historical and bodily existence, and above all the human form of Jesus, was mere semblance without any true reality."[53] That doctrine was rejected at the Nicene Council. The Bible says that He had to defeat Satan as a man anointed by the Holy Spirit, which is found in Acts 10:38: *"How God anointed Jesus of Nazareth with the Holy Ghost and with power: who went about doing good, and healing all that were oppressed of the Devil; for God was with Him. And we are witnesses of all things which He did both in the land of the Jews, and in Jerusalem; whom they slew and hanged on a tree: Him God raised up the third day, and shewed Him openly."[54]* Jesus resolved all issues created by Adam's fall. His death on the Cross opened up a door whereby mankind can be freed from the power of Adam's sinful nature. His death and resurrection ransomed us from Satan's snare, redeemed us from the curse of the law, reconciled us back to God, and gave us the precious gift of forgiveness.

In heaven right now, there is a Man sitting on the throne. His name is Jesus Christ and He has been given dominion over all of creation. *"God, who at various times, and in various manners, spoke in time past unto the fathers by the prophets, hath in these last days spoken unto us by His Son, whom He hath appointed Heir of all things, by whom also He made the worlds."[55]*

DIVINE PRESENCE RESTS BETWEEN US

"For where two or three are gathered together in My name, I am there in the midst of them."[56] Jewish rabbis, especially of the old order, believed that when they studied the Scriptures with two of them, the Shekinah presence of God would be there in the midst of them. "When two sit together and words of Torah pass between them, the Divine Presence rests between them."[57]

What Jesus is inferring is that when two or three come together in His name and are in full agreement, there He is in the midst of them. He is the Shekinah that's in the midst of them bringing the revelation of God and Jesus. When a small group comes together in unity, it creates the Ark of the Covenant that contains the Shekinah. Not just an A-R-K but an A-R-C, a gathering together that creates a luminous discharge of revelation that will transform our minds.

Nicodemus, Pharisee and member of the ruling council, came to Jesus in the middle of the night (probably to avoid being seen by his fellow Pharisees). Nicodemus opens the dialog, recognizing that Jesus was a teacher sent from God. While talking with Jesus, suddenly, there was an arc, a connection that was formed, and the words of Jesus flowed in divine profundity. It is these words that cause Nicodemus to scratch his head: *"Most assuredly, I say to you, unless one is born again, he cannot see the kingdom of God."*[58] The literal interpretation is 'unless one is born from above' you cannot see the kingdom. You cannot see because you operate out of three dimensions. But when you are born again, then your genetic strand begins to turn on and you begin to move and operate, not just out of the natural strands of your DNA, but also the spiritual aspects so that you can begin to see beyond this dimension. Your spiritual senses can now begin to function in another realm. Without the born-again experience, man never truly knows what it means to be fully human. Apart from God, he is incomplete, as he was intended to be, in the image and likeness of God.

Your spiritual, physical, and emotional self can come into the fullness of what God created you to be. You become naturally supernatural so that you can move in both dimensions, in and out of that realm as you were always created to be. Your blood is transformed in the realm of the spirit and you become an heir, and joint heir with Christ. Everything that's in heaven and in the earth belongs to you now. God wants to take us back.

"Now when He was asked by the Pharisees when the kingdom of God would come, He answered them and said, 'The kingdom of God does not come with observation; nor will they say, "See here!" or "See there!" For indeed, the kingdom of God is within you.'"[59] Think about who He's talking to. He's talking to Pharisees that are not even born again. He is saying to the Pharisees that the kingdom of God is within you. The Amplified Bible says that it's all around you. He's speaking to Pharisees and essentially saying, "It's in you, it's in Me. It's all around us. But you just can't see it because you haven't been born again. You're still operating out of your fallen nature in your DNA. Pharisees, I must tell you something. I'm operating out of the new creation DNA." He said that the kingdom of God is within you, but you just can't see it because you're not born again. Jesus tells Nicodemus that 'flesh is born of flesh.' Flesh begets flesh, but Spirit begets spirit. When you are born again, then you are connected to the heavenly realm and that dimension empowers you to be released into all the possibilities that are given to you as one who has been born again.

Let's do a little science education. Human cells contain 23 pairs of chromosomes for a total of 46. There was something that happened inside of you that made you aware that you were born again. You didn't need to ask the preacher if you were born again. Blessed be the God and Father of our Lord Jesus Christ! First Peter 1:3 is critical for your understanding. *"According to His great mercy, He has caused us to be born again."* You knew it, without a doubt, when the new life happened. The spiritual world became real to you. You now sense it. You get a new life, not a new religion. You are introduced to the spiritual realm. You don't learn about it. You experience it. The great joy is uncovered when we are joined to Christ and made one.

8 / GENETIC TRANSFIGURATIONS, PART TWO

JACOB'S DREAMS AND MOSES' BODY

ONE OF THE INTERESTING THINGS THAT HAPPENS AFTER THE NEW BIRTH is that we experience dreams. Not those crazy, demonic, horrible dreams. Dreams that come from another realm, the realm of the Spirit. Let's look at Genesis 28:12-14:

> "Then he dreamed, and behold, a ladder was set up on the earth, and its top reached to heaven; and there the angels of God were ascending and descending on it. And behold, the Lord stood above it and said: 'I am the Lord God of Abraham your father and the God of Isaac; the land on which you lie I will give to you and your descendants. Also your descendants shall be as the dust of the earth; you shall spread abroad to the west and the east, to the north and the south; and in you and in your seed all the families of the earth shall be blessed.'"

Leaving Isaac, Jacob sets out on the way to Haran. Night began to overtake him, and sleep overwhelmed him. He was probably far from any dwelling. He had no choice but to lay down there and get ready to sleep. He dreams. A ladder or stairs are seen reaching from earth to heaven, on which angels ascend and descend. The expression "the angel of God" is common, but that of "the angels of God" is most rare. We suppose that the sleeper's eyes were revealed to the heavenly hosts, the members and attendants of the heavenly court. "Ascending" with tasks completed; "descending" with fresh commissions from above.[1]

Jacob is awakened with God speaking: *I am the Lord God of Abraham thy father and the God of Isaac.* What's He talking about? Genealogies, genetics, and generations. It is interesting that He does not use His personal name Jehovah, but announces Himself as the Elohim, who enters into a solemn covenant with Jacob's ancestors, and who had now come, in virtue of that covenant, to renew with Jacob the promises he had previously received. Elohim announces that He is standing over Jacob because He has something that in the fullness of time (*through My Son*) will be fully activated. The land where Jacob is laying down will be given to him. What land? The earth. To Jacob's seed. And his seed's seed shall be as the dust of the earth. There's that word, dust. Now, the seed shall spread abroad to the west and the east, and to the north and the south. And in his seed shall all the families of the earth be blessed.

Jacob was able to tap into the supernatural reality as he went into a dream state. In that place of dreaming, he was able to transcend dimensions. He saw the ladder ascending to the heavens. Now you have to understand what he was really seeing. Was it a physical ladder that he was ascending and descending? No, I believe it was a genetic code that he saw. It was the double helix strand that he was seeing, the helix that the angels were ascending and descending. They were ascending and descending off of his genetic code.

The Bible says that the kingdom of God is within you. That means you are a portal for the supernatural. When you are a new creation, son of a new birth, everything that is in the realm of the Spirit is attached to you through your genealogy, the genetic code through Jesus Christ. The supernatural thing that is in heaven, in the invisible, can come down into the natural.

The saints of the Old Testament were pressing into the kingdom that we are now freely given through Jesus Christ. Even Moses transcended his generation. When he was ascending Mount Sinai, the Bible says that something began to take place within his physical body. They had to shroud his face with a veil. *"When Moses had finished speaking with them, he put a veil over his face."*[2] Why? Why did they put a veil over his face? Because he transcended his generation. He tapped into something that wasn't even fully available, but because he went into a high place outside of time and space, he went into an eternal realm where Christ was already the Lamb slain before the foundations of the world. He was able to take hold of it and pull it into his physical body.

Imagine this: *"Moses was one hundred and twenty years old when he died. His eyes were not dim, nor his natural vigor diminished."* In fact, Exodus tells us that his face shone with the glory of God. If you study that word *shone*, you will see that it means that he grew horns. He took on the nature of God. "Some scholars believe that Jerome mistranslated the Hebrew word 'qaran.' Other scholars believe that Jerome knew exactly what he was doing. He purposely chose "cornuta" to mean "horn" as a metaphor. Because horns in the Bible are always a symbol of strength and power. Jerome wanted to convey that Moses was reflecting the strength and power of God."[3]

SATAN AND THE GENETIC CODE

Something happened to the DNA and the body of Moses. They've been looking for the body of Moses forever. They can't find it. Satan contended for that body because within that body was a genetic code that Satan wanted. He said that he wanted that body, and Michael came, and he contended with Satan. He said, "You can't have that body. I want that body because that body has the genetic code of God that's perfect."

That was one of the reasons why Satan came to Jesus Christ and tempted Him to kill him so that he could have that code. That's why he came, because he knew who He was. Satan said to Christ, "If You are the Son of God, do these things." Why did he want to do that?

Because he wanted to possess that DNA for himself. Because he recognized that if he could possess that genetic code, then he would become God over all the universe. He would exalt his throne above the heavens. That's what happened with Nimrod. He set up the Tower of Babel as a supernatural portal. During the early chapters of Genesis, there were a number of bizarre events. One of those events was the Tower of Babel. There are only a few verses in Genesis 11 that offer us the historical account of the Tower of Babel. The descendants of Noah settled in a land named Shinar. The population was growing, and they all spoke one language. At one point, they decided to build a tall tower to the skies, a proud symbol of how great they had made their nation. God came down to see what man was doing and decided that this was not good, and He confused their languages and scattered them across the nations.

The key figure in the building of the tower was Nimrod. The Babylonians wanted a tower that would "reach to the heavens" so that they could be like God and that they would not need Him. Nimrod's mother, Semiramis, consoled the people by making them believe the child she carried was Nimrod "reincarnated."[4] Through her scheming and designing, Semiramis became the Babylonian "Queen of Heaven," and Nimrod, under various names, became the "divine son of heaven." Through the generations, in this idolatrous worship, Nimrod became the false Messiah, son of Baal the Sun-god. In this false *Babylonish* system, the "Mother and Child" (Semiramis and Nimrod reborn), became chief objects of worship. This worship of 'Mother and Child' spread over the world. The names varied in different countries and languages. It is interesting that in Egypt, it was Isis and Osiris.[5]

This historical background of Nimrod makes it clear that he was the first antichrist and I believe that he held within himself a Satanic code, and many believe that he was one of the very leaders of the Nephilim agenda on the planet. Let's just use some common sense here: if the height of the tower was so important, then why would you build it in a valley? It doesn't make any sense. The real issue is that it might be a supernatural portal. Possessed by Satan, Nimrod wanted to take the DNA of the other god and he would bring down God if possible. Does this sound familiar? *"For thou hast said in thine heart, I will ascend into heaven, I will exalt my throne above the stars of God: I will sit also upon the mount of the congregation, in the sides of the north: I will ascend above the heights of the clouds; I will be like the most High."*[6] As with Lucifer, Nimrod failed. That's why God said to Himself, "We've got to go down and confuse their language."

THE POWER OF A SEED

"Being born again, not of corruptible seed, but of incorruptible, by the word of God, which liveth and abideth forever."[7]

If you are going to be a student of the Scriptures, you can't just read the Bible, you must study it. Paul gave young Timothy some great advice: *"Study to shew thyself approved unto God, a workman that needeth not to be ashamed, rightly dividing the word of truth."*[8] Look intuitively into the Scriptures and prove yourself that you are a student of the word.

The Scriptures speak to the intense research and inquiry that the prophets made concerning the coming of the Christ. Peter referred to this prophetic searching which even the angels were looking into: *"Of this salvation the prophets have inquired and searched carefully, who prophesied of the grace that would come to you trying to find out the time and circumstances to which the Spirit of Christ in them was pointing when he predicted the sufferings of the Messiah and the glories that would follow. It was revealed to them that they were not serving themselves but you, when they spoke of the things that have now been told to you by those who have preached the gospel to you by the Holy Spirit sent from heaven. Even angels long to look into these things."* The two Greek words, *inquired* and *searched*, give a much livelier picture than the English, of the intense eagerness of the search, and of the depth to which it penetrated. If these great prophets took such pains to understand our present salvation, we ought to take heed not to 'let it slip.'[9]

Did you know that even Daniel studied the star system to find out when Jesus Christ was going to come to the earth? *"Know and understand this: From the time the word goes out to restore and rebuild Jerusalem until the Anointed One."*[10] The later Magi, especially those in Babylon and Persia (where the influence of Daniel, as well as Mordecai and Esther) had been profound and long-lasting, would surely be familiar with this prophecy and also the various prophecies of Daniel

Daniel knew when Jesus Christ would come to the earth. It appears that the Magi could be of the order of Daniel. Daniel studied astronomy, not astrology. Astrology is the worship of the stars. Astronomy is the study of the stars. He could tell the times and the seasons by the stars. And the Magi knew because it had all been mapped out by Daniel, indicating when the Christ was going to come. Everyone knew, even Herod knew. That's why he was looking to kill the babies. They knew, and so when they saw the star, then they brought the gifts to Jesus because they understood that it was the time. Stars are aligning. That's why Jesus Christ is *the bright and morning star.* When you start to go into that dimension, the very first thing you'll begin to see is a bright light that shines like a star. Even people that have had near death experiences say, "Well, I saw a bright light..."

That supernatural dimension belongs to us now because we are seated with Him in heavenly places, in the spirit. Your spirit is seated with Him, your soul and spirit are connected to the supernatural realm. The process of renewal and restoration in your life began when you were born again and now you have the ability by faith to go into that dimension.

"Being born again, not of corruptible seed, but of incorruptible by the Word of God, which liveth and abideth forever."[11] This is not the seed of Abraham; it is the seed of God (Ellicott's Commentary).

One last great verse to energize our thoughts: *"His seed remaineth in him; and he cannot sin, because he is born of God."*[12] John is communicating a living principle to the soul which can never decay.

You are eternal because Jesus Christ came to pay for the souls of men, so that they would have full access through their genetic code into that realm. As you go into that dimension, the things that you see in the spirit, through your soul, you're able to pull down into your physical body and make them manifest into the earth. Many people don't understand how to harvest things in the spirit.

We have the ability to open up the heavens through worship and praise and create a frequency that transcends the natural and pulls down the invisible into our realm. As the heavens open through their new creation reality, they're able to pull things that are invisible and make them come into the earth to be harvested from the unseen. Many have experienced exactly what I am talking about, the supernatural manifestations in our midst. But the body of Christ, in many ways, has not been able to harvest the unseen. They don't take advantage of the things that they pull into the earth, the supernatural revelation of things like technology that others discovered. As a result, many of the things that the church has pulled into the earth, the world has taken advantage of. Because the world doesn't operate out of spirit; their spirit is dead. They operate out of their soul.

This is going to change your life. I'm teaching you how to pull the invisible into the natural and make it manifest in every area of your life. We should be the most technologically advanced people on the planet. Here is the issue: You have a supernatural experience in the heavenly realm, and you feel the goosebumps and the presence of God, but then you never pull anything out of that realm and bring it into your soul. You must focus your mind on what you have just encountered. Pull it into you and then birth it out of you. Many times, when I am in the spiritual realm and ministering, I'll see something in the realm of the spirit that's in the room, whether it's a sign and a wonder, or whatever it is.

When supernatural events enter the room, no matter what they are, when you see them, you begin to pull them in with your soul and bring them down into your physical body and then speak them out into manifestation. That's how you do it, through your spirit. You have access to the realm of the spirit because your spirit is in those dimensions. You are seated with Christ in heavenly places. Your soul is the thing that connects the body to the spirit. That's why God created you as body, soul, and spirit. All three have to be activated. Often when we are in the space of the Holy Spirit, there are opportunities to receive spiritual revelation and see things beyond our imagination. When this happens, pull these things into the earth's atmosphere. Harvest these things, these ideas, these inventions, these things that we bring into the earth. You can do a historical study and it will show that every time there is a major move of God on the earth, there is always a corresponding technological advancement of man.

The saints of God often get revelation and divine insight, but never do anything with it. They bring it into the atmosphere but don't get it. Then, this person that is operating out of their soul is able to see something in their mind, during the night season. They wake up and remember the idea they had during the night and they think it is a great idea and they go to work to create it. Unfortunately, some of the richest people on the earth are not Christians. There was a spiritual technology that was birthed into the earth, and they were able to harvest those things and bring them into the natural and make millions of dollars off of them. The church needs to begin to harvest the things that we are pulling in.

I am going to give you five practical applications to activate your DNA and allow the government of God to rest over your life. As you go and pray and you begin to see these things, you are able to pull them into your soul and then bring them down into your physical body and release them into a reality.

NUMBER ONE: DESIRE

"Therefore, I say unto you, what things soever ye desire, when ye pray, believe that ye receive them, and ye shall have them."[13]

What you *desire* when you pray, when you're praying and you're going into the realm of the spirit, your desires become yours. It is important that we finish out the verse. Desire must be coupled with faith. Literally, it is interpreted with these words: What you desire, pray, and when you pray, have the faith of God and you will receive. I will add another verse to establish my point. *"Hope deferred makes the heart sick, but when the desire comes, it is a tree of life."*[14] A delay is disastrous and not desired. It leads to a sickness of the soul, a sinking in the heart. But when the desire is answered, it is like the tree of life, like heaven in Eden's garden, plucking heavenly fruit for the tree of life.

NUMBER TWO: PRAYING IN THE SPIRIT

"But you, beloved, building yourselves up on your most holy faith, praying in the Holy Spirit..."[15]

I will take you a little deep here as we examine a two-fold revelation in this Scripture. Most people think that it's just praying in the Spirit, praying in tongues. But there is actually another dimension where you go into the spirit and actually pray. Many of the Orthodox teachers and church fathers understood that it wasn't just praying in tongues but actually going into the spirit. Also, a lot of the saints of the Catholic Church taught about going into the spirit and praying. This is taught in the Orthodox Church. "For prayer is not man's lonely cry across empty spaces to a far-off God. Prayer is man's being in God; being in the Holy Spirit."[16] The double spirit of praying in your spirit with the Holy Spirit.

NUMBER THREE: MEDITATION

As you pray in the Spirit, a silence comes over your soul, the soul grows quiet, and the spirit begins to move. It takes discipline for us in the Western world to learn how to sit in a quiet place. When you get into the center of quiet, your spirit begins to move and dimensions open up to you. In that sweet place, you begin to pray in the Spirit. It takes restraint and requires the focus of your body, your soul, and your spirit to pull the supernatural in. I love the Psalmist's words: *"When I remember thee upon my bed and meditate on thee in the night watches."*[17] I have found in my own life and in the life of many others that supernatural encounters often happen in the night season. Many dreams, visions, voices, and other spiritual events will happen while you're at rest, because your soul (mind and emotions) are at ease. Your mind is at rest, and so it's able to transcend into heavenly dimensions. That's what happened to Jacob as his mind was at rest and he was able to tap into a supernatural dimension that he never expected.

NUMBER FOUR: THE BLOOD OF JESUS

> "Therefore, brethren, having boldness to enter the Holiest by the blood of Jesus, let us draw near with a true heart in full assurance of faith, having our hearts sprinkled from an evil conscience and our bodies washed with pure water."[18]

The blood of lambs and goats could not compare to the blood of Christ. It was a substitute. But, even as a substitute, Moses had to keep a veil over his face because of the glory shining on his face. The people couldn't receive something that wasn't available to them at that time. But the veil has now been taken away and we are able to stare straight into the very face of God and allow ourselves to be changed and transformed.

Your spirit is completely perfect. Your soul is being transformed so that it takes on the likeness of God. The image is the physical body, the likeness is the soul of man, the characteristics, the fruit of the Spirit. Become a full tree growing up and bearing much fruit. You are the fruit that will remain. It happens by applying the blood of Christ.

The god of this world did his devious work of blinding men's eyes, but the Creator of light called forth that light out of the darkness. The light of glory blinded Paul, but soon God would cause him to live in the light of that glory. The glory of the divine perfections shining in and through the Redeemer would illuminate all those that are drawn to Him and they would be a light unto the world, as well. As it was with Moses, so it is with us. We don't look the same when the light of glory emanates upon us and through us. You are a light being, and a light bearer. That's why Jesus said that we are a light sitting on a hill. The darker it is, the brighter the light of glory will shine through us.

"*They go from strength to strength, every one of them in Zion appeareth before God.*"[19] Wilhelm DeWette, the German theologian, exegetes the verse this way: "*Going they increase in strength, until they appear before God in Zion.*" This might be the best. It is a combination of interpretation and spiritual addition by the Oxford trained J.C. Philpott. "Every one of them appears before God, *washed in the Savior"s blood, clothed in the Redeemer's righteousness, adorned with all the graces of the Spirit, and made fit for the inheritance of the saints in light.*"[20]

As you travel into that holy dimension and present yourself to the God of Zion, you will be given strength as you travel along into that realm of glory.

NUMBER FIVE: COMMUNION

"The cup of blessing that we bless, is it not a participation in the blood of Christ? The bread that we break, is it not a participation in the body of Christ?"[21]

"So, Jesus said to them, 'Truly, truly, I say to you, unless you eat the flesh of the Son of Man and drink his blood, you have no life in you. Whoever feeds on my flesh and drinks my blood has eternal life, and I will raise him up on the last day.'"[22]

The eucharist, or communion as others would define the celebration of the Lord's Supper, is the center of worship for all churches, in varying times and ways of celebration. In the early church, the celebration of communion was an essential part of the Christian life.

According to Paul's words to the church at Corinth, he viewed communion as a participation in the body and blood of Christ.

Many of the early church fathers believed that the bread and wine were changed into the body and the blood of our Lord. Let's start with the voices from the early Church Fathers that advanced the truth that the bread and wine are transformed into the flesh and blood of our Lord.

ST. IGNATIUS OF ANTIOCH

St. Ignatius became the third bishop of Antioch, succeeding St. Evodius, who was the immediate successor of St. Peter. He heard St. John preach when he was a boy and knew St. Polycarp, Bishop of Smyrna. Seven of his letters written to various Christian communities have been preserved. Eventually, he received the martyr's crown as he was thrown to wild beasts in the arena.

"Consider how contrary to the mind of God are the heterodox in regard to the grace of God which has come to us. They have no regard for charity, none for the widow, the orphan, the oppressed, none for the man in prison, the hungry or the thirsty. They abstain from the Eucharist and from prayer, because they do not admit that the Eucharist is the flesh of our Savior Jesus Christ, the flesh which suffered for our sins and which the Father, in His graciousness, raised from the dead" (*Letter to the Smyrnaeans*, paragraph 6. circa 80-110 A.D.).[23]

"I have no taste for the food that perishes nor for the pleasures of this life. I want the Bread of God which is the Flesh of Christ, who was the seed of David; and for drink I desire His Blood which is love that cannot be destroyed" (*Letter to the Romans*, paragraph 7, circa 80-110 A.D.). [24]

ST. JUSTIN MARTYR

St. Justin Martyr was born a pagan but converted to Christianity after studying philosophy. He was a prolific writer and many Church scholars consider him the greatest apologist, or defender of the faith, from the 2nd century. He was beheaded with six of his companions sometime between 163 and 167 A.D.

"This food we call the Eucharist, of which no one is allowed to partake except one who believes that the things we teach are true, and has received the washing for forgiveness of sins and for rebirth, and who lives as Christ handed down to us. For we do not receive these things as common bread or common drink; but as Jesus Christ our Savior being incarnate by God's Word took flesh and blood for our salvation, so also we have been taught that the food consecrated by the Word of prayer which comes from him, from which our flesh and blood are nourished by transformation, is the flesh and blood of that incarnate Jesus" (*First Apology*, Ch. 66, inter A.D. 148-155).[25]

ST. ATHANASIUS OF ALEXANDRIA

St. Athanasius was born in Alexandria ca. 295 A.D. He was ordained a deacon in 319 A.D. He accompanied his bishop, Alexander, to the Council of Nicea, where he served as his secretary. Eventually he succeeded Alexander as Bishop of Alexandria. He is most known for defending Nicene doctrine against Arian disputes.

"The great Athanasius in his sermon to the newly baptized says this: 'You shall see the Levites bringing loaves and a cup of wine and placing them on the table. So long as the prayers of supplication and entreaties have not been made, there is only bread and wine. But after the great and wonderful prayers have been completed, then the bread becomes the Body, and the wine the Blood, of our Lord Jesus Christ.' And again: 'Let us approach the celebration of the mysteries. This bread and this wine, so long as the prayers and supplications have not taken place, remain simply what they are. But after the great prayers and holy supplications have been sent forth, the Word comes down into the bread and wine - and thus His Body is confected" (*Sermon to the Newly Baptized*, ante 373 A.D).[26]

ST. IRENAEUS

St. Irenaeus succeeded St. Pothinus to become the second bishop of Lyons in 177 A.D. Earlier in his life, he studied under St. Polycarp. Considered one of the greatest theologians of the 2nd century, St. Irenaeus is best known for refuting the Gnostic heresies.

"So then, if the mixed cup and the manufactured bread receive the Word of God and become the Eucharist, that is to say, the Blood and Body of Christ, which fortify and build up the substance of our flesh, how can these people claim that the flesh is incapable of receiving God's gift of eternal life, when it is nourished by Christ's Blood and Body and is His member? As the blessed apostle says in his letter to the Ephesians, 'For we are members of His Body, of His flesh and of His bones' (Eph. 5:30). He is not talking about some kind of 'spiritual' and 'invisible' man, 'for a spirit does not have flesh and bones' (Lk. 24:39). No, he is talking of the organism possessed by a real human being, composed of flesh and nerves and bones. It is this which is nourished by the cup, which is His Blood, and is fortified by the bread which is His Body. The stem of the vine takes root in the earth and eventually bears fruit, and 'the grain of wheat falls into the earth' (Jn. 12:24), dissolves, rises again, multiplied by the all-containing Spirit of God, and finally after skilled processing, is put to human use. These two then receive the Word of God and become the Eucharist, which is the Body and Blood of Christ" (*Five Books on the Unmasking and Refutation of the Falsely named Gnosis.* Book 4:18 4-5, circa 180 A.D.).[27]

ST. CYRIL OF JERUSALEM

St. Cyril served as Bishop of Jerusalem in the years 348-378 A.D.

"I have received from the Lord that which I also delivered unto you, that the Lord Jesus, the same night in which He was betrayed, took bread, etc. [1 Cor. 11:23]. This teaching of the Blessed Paul is alone sufficient to give you a full assurance concerning those Divine Mysteries, which when ye are vouchsafed, ye are of (the same body)

[Eph. 3:6] and blood with Christ. For he has just distinctly said, (That our Lord Jesus Christ the same night in which He was betrayed, took bread, and when He had given thanks He broke it, and said, Take, eat, this is My Body: and having taken the cup and given thanks, He said, take, drink, this is My Blood.) [I Cor. 2:23-25] Since then He Himself has declared and said of the Bread, (This is My Body), who shall dare to doubt any longer? And since He has affirmed and said, (This is My Blood), who shall ever hesitate, saying, that it is not His blood?" *(Catechetical Lectures* 22 Mystagogic).[28]

THE REAL PRESENCE OF CHRIST

The Real Presence of Christ in the Eucharist is a term used in theology that expresses the doctrine that Jesus is *really* or substantially present in the Eucharist, not merely symbolically or metaphorically, and that is similar to many of the very early church fathers. There are a number of different views in the understanding of the meaning of the term "real" in this context among contemporary Christian confessions which accept the doctrine, including Catholicism, Eastern Orthodoxy, Oriental Orthodoxy, Lutheran, Methodist, Reformed Christian, and a few others.

The teaching of the Catholic Church on transubstantiation was formulated by the teachings of St. Thomas Aquinas during the thirteenth century. This belief is expressed in this phrase: "the change of the whole substance of bread into the substance of the Body of Christ and of the whole substance of wine into the substance of his Blood. This change is brought about in the eucharistic prayer though the efficacy of the word of Christ and by the action of the Holy Spirit. However, the outward characteristics of bread and wine, that is the 'eucharistic species', remain unaltered." The manner in which the change occurs, the Roman Catholic Church teaches, is a mystery.[29]

Concerning the Eastern Orthodox Church, it is unlike the churches of the West that are immersed in history; the East is immersed in mystery. The East is more contemplative, poetic, and rich in symbol. Not that these are lacking in the West, but history has made the West more conscious of the sufferings of mankind. All the Orthodox formulas ask the Spirit to make the individual holy, transform the elements into the body and blood of Christ, etc. And so, this term is very important for an understanding of the mystery of the Church and the sacraments. The liturgy is a place to offer one's own sufferings with those of Christ. The East is rather a place where one goes to liturgy to taste "a little bit of heaven" so that one can return to everyday life with hope and a sense that the shortness of life will open onto the everlasting timelessness of heaven.[30]

The Real Presence of Christ is represented by the Lutherans, Anglicans, and Wesleyans today. However, rather than holding that the whole substance of the bread and wine is transformed (i.e. transubstantiation), they consider the body and blood to exist alongside the bread and wine—"In, with, and under the forms of bread and wine." The United Methodist Church and most of the smaller Methodist bodies believe in the Real Presence, but do not accept transubstantiation along with most Protestant denominations. The UMC refers to Christ's presence in the Eucharist as a "Holy Mystery," and prefers not to explain the details of Christ's presence.

THE GREAT MYSTERY

Communion is a great mystery that we will not fully understand until the marriage supper of the Lamb. For some, it is but a type and symbol, but for others there is a supernatural aspect to each of the sacraments. All of us have our own fixed views on the nature of Holy Communion. But, one thing is very certain: the Eucharist is mystical and will remain a mystery until we see Him face to face. "The celebration of the Lord's Supper," said Chrysostom, "is the commemoration of the greatest blessing that ever the world enjoyed."

Because of my background as well as my study, I have come to the belief that the bread and wine become Jesus: His body, blood, soul, and divinity. Even though I can't fully understand how it happens, my faith stands on this revelation, the revelation that we are partaking of Christ in the resurrection upon the throne. In the communion setting, there are those that would place their gaze upon Christ on the Cross. Throughout the communion service, they have created a sorrowful setting that focuses on the Cross rather than the resurrection, and on sorrow, rather than jubilation.

As I would position myself for receiving the elements. I fix my gaze upon His now seated place in the heavens above all rulers and principalities. In Paul's letter to the Ephesians, he wrote these words: *"...and raised us up together, and made us sit together in the heavenly places in Christ Jesus."*[31] As we partake of Holy Communion, we are participating in this revelation that we are also living from above, not beneath, and therefore living from a place of life and not death. The miracle of Communion again is a mystery, something that human reason can never really understand. Christ united thanksgiving, sacrifice, and a meal in which Christians receive the very life of God and enter into union and communion with Him.

There is an inseparable junction of sign and reality. As truly as we eat the bread and drink the wine, we feed on Christ. It is a mystery. Calvin spoke it correctly: "Now if anyone should ask me how this takes place, I shall not be ashamed to confess that it is a secret too lofty for either my mind to comprehend or my words to declare. And, to speak more plainly, I rather experience than understand."[32]

The blood holds the genetic code and when you're partaking of God's blood, you're partaking of pure light, and you're releasing and allowing that light to come into your physical body. In John 6:53-58, Jesus said to His disciples, *"Truly, truly, I say unto you, unless you eat the flesh of the son of man and drink his blood, you have no life in you. Whoever feeds on my flesh and drinks my blood has eternal life, and I will raise him up on the last day. For my flesh is true food and my blood is to drink. Whoever feeds on my flesh and drinks, my blood abides in me and I in him."*

There is a special intimacy that takes place in communion, but it only happens if it is more than just a lifeless, meaningless ceremony which happens in too many churches. A fellowship between the Holy Trinity, God the Son, God the Father, God the Holy Ghost and your spirit, soul, and body takes place as God and man enter into a spiritual affiliation of holy affection. I live because of the Son, for His blood flows through me. I feed on Him and I live because of that divine nourishment. *"I am the living bread which came down from heaven. If anyone eats of this bread, he will live forever; and the bread that I shall give is My flesh, which I shall give for the life of the world."*[33]

This is the bread that came down from heaven, not the manna that your ancestors ate and then died in the wilderness. Whoever feeds on this bread will live forever. The Pharisees argued over this statement, "How can He give us His flesh to eat?" You remember His words: "Unless you eat My flesh and drink My blood you have no life in you."

What part of you will live forever? It's your spirit and soul that lives forever. In fact, when you die, you leave your body and your soul and spirit will enter the heavenly realms, not just for a visit, but to live there forever. Jesus Christ came to save souls. So, when you participate and partake in communion, you are partaking of Christ's flesh. You are partaking of His blood and His body, and it becomes part of your natural body, your soul, and your spirit, because Jesus was body, soul, and spirit. Because He had a mind, He had a will, and He had emotions.

There are those religious groups that believed Jesus Christ was flawless and could not have sinned. If He could not have sinned, then the Word did not become flesh. He did not become one of us. In order to complete the Father's plan, Jesus had to be God and man, the two in one. Jesus walked this earth as a man completely sin free, not because He could not have sinned, but because He chose not to. Let that sink in for a moment.

A BRAND-NEW PEOPLE

"The Lord (God) says to my Lord (the Messiah), Sit at My right hand, until I make Your adversaries Your footstool. The Lord will send forth from Zion the scepter of Your strength; rule, then, in the midst of Your foes. Your people will offer themselves willingly in the day of

Your power, in the beauty of holiness and in holy array out of the womb of the morning; to You [will spring forth] Your young men, who are as the dew. The Lord has sworn and will not revoke or change it: You are a priest forever, after the manner and order of Melchizedek."[34]

David was seeing something that transcended his time. The Lord, the Messiah, Jesus Christ sitting on the throne! On the day of Christ's manifest power, there will be a people who will not be offering goats and lambs, but will offer themselves as a holy sacrifice to the Messiah. They will not be priests after the order of the Levitical priesthood. They will be priests after a different order, the order of Melchizedek. That is an eternal priesthood, that is the priests in the heavenly realms.

Your blood is now Father's blood, and you have been disconnected from your earthly genealogy and are now connected to a spiritual genealogy through the Lamb that was slain from the foundation of the world. David saw this. He prophetically saw this in the heavenly realm, before it ever transpired. He saw Christ the Messiah take His seat in the eternal realm. How did Father God respond? *"I'm going to reverse earthly and heavenly orders. God said, 'Sit down, My Son, My Love. I'm going to make Your enemies Your footstool'."*

Beyond that, God says that there will be a people that are going to mirror His Son's image and will be in His likeness. They will rise out of the womb of the morning. There will be a spiritual rebirth and they will not be of a natural order. They will be after the order of Melchizedek, without mother or father and without human genealogy. *"For we are members of His body, of His flesh, and of His bones."*[35]

9 / TRANSFIGURATION

THE 4 ORDERS OF SUPERNATURAL TRAVEL

"And it came to pass about eight days after these sayings, he took Peter and John and James, and went up into a mountain to pray. And as he prayed, the fashion of his countenance was altered, and his raiment was white and glistening."[1]

E.M. BOUNDS, THE PRODIGIOUS PREACHER AND ILLUSTRIOUS TEACHER, put the pen in his hand and wrote these words: "He had wrapped Himself up in a bit of human tapestry so He could move among men without blinding their eyes. Now, He looks out through the strands. They are astonished and awed to find that face they know so well now shining as the sun, and the garments made transparent as light, glistening like snow, by reason of the great brilliance of the light within. Yet, Jesus let out only a part of the glory."[2]

On a mountaintop, Jesus prayed while His disciples were heavy with sleep. A flash of light awakens them. Jesus stood before them, transfigured, metamorphosed by His glory. The fashion of His countenance altered, becoming other than what it had been. As the disciples gazed, Jesus' form and features shone with a new glory, strikes of lightning as from an inward radiance, bright as the sun, as though He was wrapped with the Shekinah cloud. Even His garments were "white as the light," "white as snow." The Word made flesh allows for a brief space for His essential glory to illuminate and shine through the apparel of a servant which He wore.

THE TRANSFIGURATION

The Greek word "*Metamorphao*" means transform or transfigure. Both Matthew and Mark use the same word in Matthew 17:2 and Mark 9:21. Luke the Physician did not use the word "transfiguration," but his writing is similar to the Greek word. It reads this way: "the appearance of His face changed."

Transfiguration is a complete change of form or appearance into a more beautiful state; it also can be said that it is where a saint's or believer's physical body, including their face, begins to glow, and a light might even compass around them and their entire body.

Beams of light may proceed out of their physical clothing, or even their pores. The Catholic Church would call this "*luminous phenomenon.*" There are five conditions the church requires to validate that this phenomenon was kept very sacred. They did not want to diminish the reality of a supernatural experience. They expected that the experiences would be validated and be a sacred and holy experience for those who had them.

During the 18th Century, Pope Benedict came up with five classifications, five conditions that would distinguish whether this was a true mystical phenomenon of transfiguration.

Number one: "Did the phenomenon take place in full daylight, or during the night? If the event took place at night, was the light more brilliant than any other lights?" That's the first condition. They wanted to eliminate exaggerations and someone trying to make a name for themselves.

Number two: "Was the light a mere spark, or was it prolonged so that the observer had time to gaze upon the person and become convinced of its reality?" They wanted to be sure that the light was not confused with a light from a natural source, like a lamp or streetlight. Also, "Did the phenomenon take place more than once?" This was really important when it came to distinguish this particular manifestation of transfiguration. They wanted to make sure that it wasn't just a one-time deal. Some of the stories I'll share from church history were more than a one-time occurrence.

Such powerful experiences cannot be relegated only to the saints of the first century or the mystics of the first 12 centuries. If it happened for them, it could happen to others in any generation, even ours. There are times when one is so close to the presence of God that their faces will begin to set aglow. It is the resemblance of Christ in them, the hope of glory which would begin to manifest, as has happened to others who had transformation experiences.

Number three: "Was the light produced during a religious act, in ecstasy, a sacred personal time, a sermon, or a prayer? It would then possess a religious nature to it." It had to have taken place during a session of prayer, where they were caught up in an ecstatic state; or they were taking the Eucharist, or in church or mass, and the person or saint would begin to illuminate light.

Saint Teresa of Avila would be so caught up in the glory and enraptured in the realms of the Spirit. Many times, only at hearing the name of "Jesus," she would have a manifestation of the illumination that would project out of her.

Number four: "Since God does not permit such manifestations to satisfy vague curiosity, but only for the good of souls, therefore, the event must be beneficial or the intervention of divine grace or lasting conversion." God does not manifest in someone's life so they can have a story to tell others. I have said this, many times. There is always a reason behind the sign and the wonder.

The Catholic Church, in particular, was very adamant about any manifestation drawing attention to the particular person. The rule was: point them to Jesus. And we need to take that same stance in the charismatic churches. We should question ourselves in this way. "Is this edifying? Is this exhorting? Is this uplifting? Is this pointing to Jesus, or is this pointing to a particular person? Is this manifestation truly from the Lord?" Anything from the Lord is always going to point people to Him, never to ourselves. I have noticed that with the mystics of the past and even in the Catholic and Eastern Orthodox

Church, you will discover that their direction is always pointing away from themselves toward Jesus. I cannot emphasize this enough.

Number five: "Are the light rays associated with a person who is holy and virtuous?" The source and the character of the one who claims a supernatural experience is vitally important. There are people who claim to have manifestations and incredible encounters, but it is always important to research them. Are they a Christian or are they involved in the occult? Are they exalting themselves or Christ?

THE SAINTS AND MYSTICAL EXPERIENCES

There are many who have been drawn to the mystical side of the saints, because their spirituality carried a depth of character and diverse experiences in the supernatural, for which many have longed for, including myself. Mesmerized by their heavenly experiences, I pined for the same closeness they shared with God. I have always pursued the mystic way, longing for experiences in the presence of God and desiring the supernatural in the heavenly places. The stories of the saints and their mystical experiences are appealing to all who seek something deeper in God.

Saint Catherine of Siena is one of the saints that you should study. She was a woman of great passion, courage, and love of God. She was drawn to the supernatural and she was skilled at resolving divisions in the church. She was highly admired for her devotion to Christ, her love of others, and her experiences in the supernatural. At the age of six, she began to receive mystical visions which, in some cases, allowed her to see guardian angels just as clearly as other people. Through these divine gifts, at her young age, Catherine vowed to give her life entirely to God. She spent days and nights of her time in total solitude, except for her confessor. Her days and night were employed in delightful exercises in contemplation, whose fruits resulted in supernatural lights, a most ardent love of God and a zeal to convert sinners.

Once, she had an encounter at the morning Mass that a Catholic priest was involved with. Following this marvel, a strange occurrence took place. She seemed to raise several inches off the ground from the altar. The Bishop Raymond writes, "I can't remember whether she came to rest down again, but her face was brilliant with light, and I was absolutely dumbfounded." Saint Catherine of Siena transfigured during Holy Mass, and actually levitated off the ground.

Saint Teresa of Avila was a Spanish mystic and a Carmelite nun. Many have said that the very name of "Jesus" would throw her into an ecstatic experience, and different manifestations would take place. Teresa had multiple visions, times of ecstasy, and moments when the Trinity appeared. In her writings, Teresa wrote about times when she understood the words the Lord spoke. The three divine persons would be with her soul in grace. She saw them within herself. She continued to say that it seemed that the three persons were so fixed on her soul that she could see the divine company.[3]

They say that Saint Joseph of Cupertino would literally levitate off the ground during a simple Mass. When he would take the Eucharist, he would begin to levitate off the ground, in the sight of all. He felt that these experiences were because of his divine union with Christ and because of his very compassion and love for God. His passion drove him to a place where he was no longer able to hide what was taking place behind closed doors.

There is another saint that illustrates my point. St. Gerard Majella was known as a "wonder worker" of his day. He once fell into an ecstasy and became so inflamed with love of God that rays began to spread throughout his entire body. Observers reported that the brilliance from this phenomenon was such that the room in which he was praying appeared to be on fire, and literally, the entire room seemed to be burning with fire.

Now, this brings us to another offshoot of transfiguration, which is what they call "incendium amoris," or "the fire of love." This is when a person's body supernaturally heats up and the body literally begins to look like it's on fire.

I remember one particular prayer meeting that was years ago. Brynn and I had just recently been married. We would go to this church and there were lots of young believers, and we would do these all-night prayer meetings. I remember one particular time when we were in the midst of prayer, and the power and presence of God came in an unusual way. Brynn, literally, began to scream at the top of her lungs. She was burning like fire and her whole body was aflame. This was years and years ago and we had no idea what was really transpiring. We were young and had no concept of what was happening because we had never read any works on the saints like Saint Gerard or Saint Teresa of Avila, or Richard Rolle who wrote a book on the fire of love.

Being Pentecostal believers, we had no idea what was transpiring. Later on, we would come to understand that she was having a manifestation of the fire of God's love. She was caught up in an ecstatic realm. If you touched her, you could feel the heat coming off of her body. She was on fire. Later on, I studied some of the saints and I realized that her event was a manifestation of 'incendium amoris.' It might not have been a full transfiguration, but it was as close as you can get.

Incendium amoris could be compared to these words of John the Baptist: "He will baptize you with the Holy Ghost and fire." These words are in the context of the words of John: "There's One greater than I that's coming." The fire, there's something about the fire. Some of the saints believe that that was incendium amoris, a manifestation of cleansing that would transpire in the lives of many of the saints.

One of those saints was Richard Rolle. Richard Rolle was heralded as one of the great English mystics of the Middle Ages. Rolle's religious adventures have been venerated since the 14th century. In *The Fire of Love*, Rolle describes his divine encounters by dividing the nature of the experience into three unique stages.

Rolle describes the first stage as the sensation of spiritual fire, a glowing presence accompanied by a feeling of physical warmth in his chest. Rolle says that the second stage is marked by an overwhelming sense of peace and joy, a taste of sweetness in his soul. Finally, Rolle explains how in the third stage, the glorious song of angels resounds, signifying his union with God's divine love.[4]

Here is some of Rolle's personal testimony upon the first time he experienced *incendium amoris*: "I cannot tell you how surprised I was the first time I felt my heart begin to warm. It was real warmth, too, not imaginary, and it felt as if it were actually on fire. I was astonished at the way the heat surged up, and how this new sensation brought great and unexpected comfort. I had to keep feeling my breast to make sure there was no physical reason for it! But once I realized that it came entirely from within, I was absolutely delighted and wanted my love to be even greater."[5]

JESUS AND THE MOUNT OF TRANSFIGURATION

Before we explore the event on the Mount of Transfiguration, I want to clarify one point that I sense is essential to our thinking before we move forward. Most believers will approach this mountain event as if the story of Jesus and the revelation of His deity and that His experiences would never be ours. Acts 10:38 says that God anointed Jesus with the Holy Spirit and power. Jesus went about doing good and healing all that were possessed with the devil. Do you believe that you can do all that Jesus did? I do. In fact, Jesus said we could do all that He did and more. These are His exact words: *"Even the least among you can do all that I have done, and greater things."*[6] Now that you have that point, *let's climb a mountain!*

Here is the whole story from Matthew's point of view in Matthew 17:1-8: *"Now after six days Jesus took Peter, James, and John, the brother of James, and led them up on a high mountain by themselves; and He was transfigured before them. His face shone like the sun, and His clothes became as white as the light. And behold, Moses and Elijah appeared to them, talking with Him. Then Peter answered and said to Jesus, 'Lord, it is good for us to be here; if You wish, let us make here three tabernacles: one for You, one for Moses, and one for Elijah.'*

"While he was still speaking, behold, a bright cloud overshadowed them; and suddenly a voice came out of the cloud, saying, 'This is My beloved Son, in whom I am well pleased. Hear Him!' And when the disciples heard it, they fell on their faces and were greatly afraid. But Jesus came and

touched them and said, 'Arise, and do not be afraid.' When they had lifted up their eyes, they saw no one but Jesus only."

The first thing that we need to look at is location. The Bible says that Jesus went to a high mountain for only one reason: to find a place of prayer. It is quite possible that He has been here before or on some other mountain for the purpose of prayer. Jesus has gone many times to a mountain or a desert to be alone and pray. Remember that the first of the five things that validate a transformation is prayer, not that Jesus needs validation. He was going to a place of seclusion to be alone and to seek God. In the midst of that seclusion, this manifestation takes place.

Now, do I believe that this was the first time that this manifestation had ever transpired? No, I believe that it took place many times, but this was the first time that the disciples went with Him. On that visit, the three—James, Peter and John—are a part of the audience to observe the transformation that included Moses, Elijah, and Jesus. Oh, and there was the voice of God that was present. Of course, Peter had to jump into the conversation and suggest that they build three tabernacles. This is sort of funny. While Peter is still jabbering away, God speaks. Peter shuts up, so God can speak. The manifestation ends, the cloud of God lifts, and the disciples fall to ground in absolute fear. Concerned, Jesus touches the three of them and they lift their eyes and all they see is Jesus.

Peter wanted to build three tabernacles, but the only thing that actually mattered was Jesus. The truth is that whatever tabernacles we make for us or others, we have missed the point. It is all about Jesus and nobody else. Jesus only.

MANIFESTED GLORY

"Indeed, in view of this fact, what once had splendor the glory of the Law [in the face of Moses] has come to have no splendor at all, because of the overwhelming glory that exceeds and excels it [the glory of the gospel in the face of Jesus Christ]. For if that which was but passing and fading away came with splendor, how much more must that which remains and is permanent abide in glory and splendor!"[7]

The law, and the total Mosaic dispensation, was only types and shadows, which ceased when the antitype and substance of Christ came. When Christ came, the old priesthood changed. The glory of the past is now lost and swallowed up by the glory of the present. The glory of the law is now subject to the glory of the gospel of good news. We have such a glorious hope, such joyful and confident expectation, we speak very freely, openly, and fearlessly of the excelling glory. We do not act like Moses who put a veil over his face, so the Israelites may not gaze upon the vanishing of the splendor that had been upon him. In fact, their minds were grown hard and callous, they became dull and lost the power of understanding. The same veil covers their hearts, so they cannot see the glory of the gospel and the face of Christ.

Now, look at 2 Corinthians 3:17-18, *"Now the Lord is the Spirit, and where the Spirit of the Lord is, there is liberty. And all of us with unveiled faces because we continue to behold the Word of God as in a mirror, the glory of the Lord are constantly being transfigured into his very own image, from ever increasing splendor and from one degree of glory to another, for this comes from the Lord who is the Spirit."*

Veiled faces, Unveiled faces, but a change has come. When Moses turned to speak to God, the veil was removed. When Israel turns to Christ, the veil will come off.

The unveiled countenance received the radiation of the divine glory. With the new creation, we have been given the ability for a lasting transfiguration that goes from one degree of glory to another degree of glory, from one splendor of the glory to a greater splendor of the glory. The verb is the same *metemorphôthè* as that used in the account of our Lord's transfiguration in Matthew 17 and it is the same verb in Romans 8:29: *"For those God foreknew He predestined to be conformed to the image of His Son."* We are the houses of God, because we are the ones that are the containers of God. He is living in us, and no other religion can say that God lives in them. They may claim to know God, they may claim to interact with God, but the difference between every other religion and Christianity is that Christianity, at its core, is Christ living in us.

"*To them, God willed to make known what are the riches of the glory of this mystery among the Gentiles: is Christ in you, the hope of glory.*" The glory that is within us, according to Colossians 1:27, is manifesting through us, and we no longer have to cover ourselves. We have been given an opportunity to be unmasked for all to see the wonder of Christ in us.

Colossians 1:28-29, "*That we may present every person mature (full-grown, fully initiated, complete, and perfect) in Christ (the Anointed One). For this I labor [unto weariness], striving with all the superhuman energy which He so mightily enkindles and works within me.*"

Paul is energized by the opportunity to bring all to Christ and he works and strives with "superhuman energy," out-raying through the believer. I love 2 Corinthians 3:11 in the Amplified: "*As in a mirror, the glory of the Lord, we are constantly being transfigured into his very own image, in ever increasing splendor and from one degree of glory to another degree of glory.*" In the "ever increasing splendor," we are being transfigured and we are given the opportunity to fully manifest our sonship in Christ on the earth.

These saints got the picture. The revelation is clear. They were dedicated and consecrated to the glory of transfiguration and were empowered by the Spirit of liberty. They were cultivating this life of contemplative prayer, they were nurturing this life of living for Christ, they were growing in this life of searching the Scripture, and they were promoting this life of gazing into the glory of God, so much so that they are being transformed into glory and it will be manifest in their physical body.

Again, the path to transfiguration is the path of centering prayer in the quiet place. There is an ascension, spiritually and physically, up into the mountain of the Lord. There is a company of people that are hungry for that transfiguration. I can hear their voices. "Not only am I going to ascend the hill of the Lord, the mountain of God, not only am I going to go spiritually into Mount Zion, like Christ, in the natural, I'm going to find a secluded place in a mountain and I'm going to begin to pray and seek the Lord."

Like Jesus, they are cultivating this on a daily basis and there was a physical manifestation that began to transpire. It was manifested in the presence of the Lord. When they go to pray, they are going to the mountain.

Secondly, they recognized, as a direct result of consistent prayer, while maintaining the rhythm of prayer, the glory would come. It is the glory that will bring the transfiguration.

These verses changed my life, and I quote them a lot. Colossians 1:26-27: "*This mystery, which was hidden for ages from generations, from angels and men, but is now revealed to his holy people, the saints, to whom God was pleased to make known how great for the Gentiles are the riches of glory, the mystery, which is Christ in you, the hope of glory.*" In verse 29, it says, "*For this I labor unto weariness, striving with all superhuman energy, which he so mightily kindles and works within me.*" This superhuman energy was coming as a result of Christ in you, the hope of glory.

"This was so that, by two unchangeable things, His promise, His oath, in which it was impossible for God to ever prove false or deceive us. We who have fled to Him for refuge might have mighty indwelling strength and strong encouragement to grasp and hold fast the hope approaching us that is set before us. Now we have this hope as a sure and steadfast anchor of the soul. It cannot slip, it cannot break down under whatsoever steps upon it, a hope that reaches further, entering into the very certainty of the presence, which is within the veil, where Christ has entered for us an advance, a forerunner, having come as a high priest forever after the order of Melchizedek."[8]

We have entered in beyond the veil. The "veil" refers to the second veil, the veil that divided the Holy Place and the Most Holy Place. At the death of Christ on the Cross, that veil was rent in two, and a way was made available for all to now enter beyond the veil.

Inside the veil is the unseen, eternal reality of the heavenly world. What is beyond the veil can begin to manifest out of the veil. What was hidden is now revealed, and what was covered can now begin to be manifested. This treasure, life within and without the veil, is for all believers that are desperately hungry for the presence of God, and for the glory of God.

Remember that transfiguration is not ultimate glorification; transfiguration is a precursor for what God is going to reveal fully at the glorification of His bride. Paul speaks of Christ in you, the hope of glory, and it is at this moment when we will experience incredible manifestations.

> "And behold that very day two of the disciples were going to the village called Emmaus, several miles from Jerusalem, and they were talking to each other about all these things that had occurred, and while they were conversating and discussing together, Jesus himself caught up with them and was already accompanying them, but their eyes were held so that they did not recognize Him."[9]

The two disciples were traveling on the road leading to Emmaus and they were discussing the events over the last few days, mainly concerning the death of their Messiah.

Suddenly, Jesus appeared on the road with them, in a *different form*. And He said to them, "What is this discussion you are having?" And they stood still, looking sad and downcast, and one of them, named Cleopas, answered Him, "Do you alone dwell as a stranger in Jerusalem, as if not knowing the things that have occurred here these days?" And He said to them, "What kind of things?" One of them told Him that they were talking about Jesus of Nazareth, who was a prophet, mighty in work and in deed, before God and all the people, and how the Chief Priest and the rulers gave Him up to be sentenced to death and crucified Him.

They did not recognize Jesus because He appeared in a different form. Jesus' physical features were held from them so that they did not recognize Him. Verse 28 picks up the final part of their conversation: *"As they drew near to the village to which they were going, he acted as if he would go no further, but they urged and insisted, saying to him, 'Remain with us towards the evening, and the day is now far spent.'"* So, He went and stayed with them. It occurred that as He reclined at the table with them, He took a loaf of bread, praised God, and gave thanks, asking for a blessing. Then He broke it and gave it to them. It is during communion that their eyes were instantly opened, and they clearly recognized Him, and He vanished, departing in their sight.

Verse 32 is the final word and the key comment of the whole conversation: "And they said to one another, *'Were not our hearts greatly moved and burning?'"* This is a burning of transformation. Their hearts were burning during the whole conversation on the road to Emmaus. Jesus went through a transformation, appearing in a different form, and that is why they did not initially recognize Him.

There they are at the table, breaking bread, and it is at that moment that their eyes are opened, and they recognize Jesus. Remember that they were telling Jesus about His crucifixion? While they were at the table, Jesus took the bread and broke it, a reminder of Christ on the Cross. Their hearts were burning. Jesus broke bread with them and then He disappeared. The burning heart created a moment of illumination that was a powerful moment, a moment of unveiling. They recognized Jesus. There was no time to talk anymore because Jesus disappeared. I wonder if we put more focus on communion, would we experience more supernatural occurrences?

MYSTICAL STORIES OF SAINT PATRICK

Saint Patrick's Church is located in Northern Ireland. I've been there. When you go to Saint Patrick's prayer room, the visitors will see a story on the wall. It is a story that is almost unbelievable, but you must believe because it has been documented by the Church. This may blow some of you away, but during the time of Saint Patrick, he was challenging many of the wicked warlocks and occultists that were pervasive across Ireland. He was really decimating the occultic practices across that entire island to the point where he banished even snakes. The reason for his actions were because a young girl had been bitten by a snake and died. This story has an unbelievable ending. Saint Patrick resurrected the young girl from the dead, and then he went about the business of banishing all the snakes on the island.

But there is a part of the story that was so inconceivable as I read it. I went on this journey to Northern Ireland because I wanted to spend some time at one of the early churches in Ireland, the Church of Saint Patrick, the church of the great mystic. On the wall, there was another story that shocked me. While St. Patrick was traveling through the wilderness, there were a number of warlocks that wanted to kill Saint Patrick, along with his disciples. By a word of knowledge, Saint Patrick knew what was going on. He had his Bible and started reading Psalm 23:

"The Lord is my shepherd, I shall not lack, he maketh me lie down in green pastures, leads me by still waters, he restores my soul. He leads me in the path of righteousness for his namesake. Yes, though I walk through the valley of the shadow of death, I shall fear no evil, for thou art with me, your rod and your staff will comfort me. You shall prepare a table before me, in the presence of my enemies, you anoint my head with oil, my cup runs over, surely goodness and mercy shall follow me all the days of my life, and lead me all the days of my life to the house of the Lord, and in his presence shall be my dwelling place."

Then, St. Patrick read this verse to his disciples: "*Even as the deer pants for the water brook, so does my soul pant for God.*" This part is a little out there, but the story is true, according to the story on the wall. After reading the verse, he prays that the Lord would hide them and that his enemies would see St. Patrick and his disciples as deer. So, the Lord hid them and made them appear as deer to these warlocks. They passed right by them and the warlocks believed that they were deer. The more you think about this story, you have to reach the conclusion that they were transfigured or morphed into deer to the enemies of God.

They were expecting a real luminescent manifestation of the light of God to come out of them. We know that God can do the miraculous when it is needed. Saint Patrick was not bound by religion and tradition. God took care of His children, in a most unusual way.

THE REVELATION TRANSFIGURATION

"When I turned to see that there was a voice that spoke to me, turning I saw seven golden lampstands, in the midst of the lampstands, one like the son of man, clothed of the robe which reached to his feet and his girdle, gold about his breast, his head and his hair were white like wool, stow, his eyes, flashing like flames of fire, his feet glowing like burnished bronze, as a refined in a furnace, and his voice was like the sound of many waters. In his right hand, he held seven stars, and from his mouth came forth a sharp two-edged sword, and his face was like the sun shining in full power in midday. When I saw him, I fell at his feet as dead."[10]

Different setting but similar event. The ensuing display will capture John's attention, probably stunned by the appearance of Christ. The spectacular drama begins with the appearance of Jesus to John the Apostle on the island of Patmos. On the Lord's day, he hears a booming voice. Then, John sees the voice and turns. It is Jesus.

Jesus is transfigured in a totally different way. Jesus took on another form. John definitely has never seen Jesus in this setting, nor this resemblance. He is clothed with a robe and a golden girdle, eyes flashing with flames of fire, feet glowing like burnished bronze, voice like the sound of many waters. He has a sword coming out of His mouth, flames of fire coming out of Him, and His countenance shone like the sun. This was a totally different appearance, a different transfiguration.

"Then I saw a Lamb, looking as if it had been slain, standing at the center of the throne, encircled by the four living creatures and the elders. The Lamb had seven horns and seven eyes, which are the seven spirits of God sent out into all the earth."[11]

In Revelation 5, Jesus is manifested, transfigured into a Lamb. We know that Jesus was revealing His nature as the Son of God. When you consider the emphasis that has been placed on 'Christ in you,' you understand that we could transfigure in similar fashion. The Christ of the fiery eyes and the Lamb of God lives inside us. It's Christ *in you,* the glorified Christ, the sword, the fiery eyes, that Christ is living on the inside of us, and we are a part of His body.

As sons and daughters of the kingdom, part of His body, and as Christ in us, we could have a moment of transfiguration while we are in the place of prayer. We partake of the riches of the glory of Christ and we long for that glory to be manifested. The veil has been ripped, torn in two, and we now have total access into the splendor and the majesty that will be revealed in and through us.

THE LIGHT OF THE GLORY

"For what we preach is not ourselves, but Jesus Christ as Lord, and ourselves [merely] as your servants (slaves) for Jesus' sake. For God Who said, Let light shine out of darkness, has shone in our hearts so as [to beam forth] the Light for the illumination of the knowledge of the majesty and glory of God [as it is manifest in the Person and is revealed] in the face of Jesus Christ (the Messiah)."[12]

First, take heed to Paul's word. We do NOT preach ourselves, but we preach Christ. We are not the object of our preaching. Christ is the object. Now, we can move on. The god of this world did his work of blinding, but the God of all worlds did His work of illuminating. "The God who at the creation bade the light to shine out of darkness, is he who has shined into our hearts; or it is the same God who has illuminated us, who commanded the light to shine at the creation."[13]

Paul says that the glory is within us, the treasure is in us, and it's wanting to be revealed and released. Let's look at 2 Corinthians 4:18: *"Since we consider and look not to the things that are seen but to the things that are unseen; for the things that are visible are temporal (brief and fleeting), but the things that are invisible are deathless and everlasting."* This is a powerful passage because this is what the saints of old were constantly doing: they were not looking at the things which are seen, but the things which are unseen. When you peek into the unseen, you will behold Christ. God and the things of His world, which are unseen and eternal, cannot be discovered by man; they must be revealed by the Holy Spirit. You might say that the eternal is hidden underneath the temporary. Seek and you will find.

"But we all, with unveiled face, beholding as in a mirror the glory of the Lord, are being transformed into the same image from glory to glory, just as by the Spirit of the Lord.' The light of creation is the same light that is within us. The eternal and majestic light unlocks and uncovers the knowledge of the majesty and glory of God, the glory that is revealed in the face of Jesus Christ, the Messiah. When the heart turns to the Lord, the veil is taken away and the light can shine.

The out-ray of the glory of God manifested in Genesis 1, who is Christ, is holding all things together, as written in Hebrews 1:3: *"He is the sole expression of the glory of God, the light being, the out-raying radiance of the divine, he is the perfect imprint, the very image of God, the nature upholding and maintaining and guiding and propelling the universe by his mighty word of power. When he had by offering himself accomplished our cleansing of sin and radiance of guilt, he sat down at the right hand of the majesty, divine majesty on high."*[14]

The sole expression of the glory of God, the light being, the out-raying radiance of the divine, is the perfect imprint, the very image of God and God's nature. Christ, the essential being of the Father, is stamped with His image. The light of the Father is His Son.

Going back to 2 Corinthians 3:18: *"And all of us, with unveiled face, are being continually beholding the word of God as in a mirror, the glory of the Lord are constantly being transfigured into his very own image, from ever increasing splendor, from one degree of glory to another degree of glory, for this comes from the spirit of the Lord.*" When you reflect on these words, you begin to realize that the out-raying glory that took place in Genesis 1 is the same glory that begins to manifest through sons and daughters when they have those moments of transfiguration.

People have asked me if we can activate a transfiguration. The answer is *no*. I believe they are of a divine nature, reserved for God to act. The saints of old postured themselves, so that they might experience a transfiguration.

Number one: The intention and desire of the heart is important. What are your intentions? Why do you want to have this manifestation? God said, "I'll give you the desires of your heart," but it is bound to your intention.

Number two: The raising of your spiritual frequency is helpful. Part of that spiritual frequency is to posture yourself so that your physical body is aligned with what is going on in your spirit. So, how do I do that? Faith is key. I believe everything is done by faith.

Number three: Obedience to the Word of God. *"Jesus said to them, 'My food is to do the will of him who sent me and to accomplish his work.'"*[15] Jesus is the supreme example of how to live a life of obeying God.

Number four: Be careful what you watch. In other words, don't put your eyes on everything; be careful what your eyes behold.

Number five: Worship! I believe all manifestations flow out of worship. By the way, you can never choose the manifestation, but it's through worship that manifestations can happen.

Number six: Fasting will always be a key to any spiritual exercise. I believe fasting is important and I believe fasting will align you to certain manifestations.

Number seven: Waiting upon God in the silent place has always been the place for the mystics and it will be for you. You can't sit and hope that some spiritual encounter and manifestation will drop in your lap. Follow the ways of Moses and Jesus and find a private place where you can be still in the center of a quiet place. Prayer and contemplation, as you wait on God, will open up doors to the supernatural and provide the necessary blueprint. In the place of contemplation, behold Christ with an unveiled face and let the glory come in.

"But we have this treasure in earthen vessels, that the excellence of the power may be of God and not of us."[16] In this frail body, this jar of clay, we have the treasure of the knowledge and experience of the glory of the Lord and God's strengthening grace. We humble ourselves in total understanding that the excellency of the power of Christ comes from the throne of God.

"Who being the brightness of his glory, and the express image of his person, and upholding all things by the word of his power, when he had by himself purged our sins, sat down on the right hand of the Majesty on high."[17] From the words of the Nicene Creed, "God of God, *Light of Light,* Very God of Very God." The glory of Christ and the perfections of God shine forth as a ray of light from the sun, reflected splendor, transfigured on the holy mountain. The essence of Christ shows forth the perfect DNA of God, exhibiting the properties of God and stamped with His image.

We have become partakers of the divine nature, God's Son, the Christ living in us. Any transfiguration will result in becoming like Christ. That nature can be different as it was with Jesus, enveloped in a glorious light or feet like bronze glowing in a furnace.

This is a fascinating documented story of Sadhu Sundar Singh. He was in Canada where he was preaching. While there in those meetings, he went to a woman's house, knocked on her front door, and they opened the door. Looking at Sundar, they were stunned. They had mistaken him for Christ because his face illuminated with such glory that they thought it was actually Jesus, just the way they pictured him.

I return to Paul's story on the road to Damascus. On that road, Paul had a profound encounter with Jesus, the One he hated. Jesus did not appear as He did with the two disciples on the road to Emmaus. Two encounters with Jesus, but both were quite different.

In the first encounter with Jesus, on the road to Emmaus, they did not recognize Him. In the second encounter, on the road to Damascus, Paul encountered Jesus, but He appeared as a beaming ball of fiery light, like the light in the beginning of creation. Paul was blinded for three days. A transfiguration can appear in different ways.

I remember a particular meeting I was at in the Middle East, and in the midst of that meeting, this woman started crying hysterically. She looked at my face and my face did not look like my face. She spoke out, "Your face looks like the face of Jesus. I see Jesus superimposed on your face." It was an incredible and dramatic manifestation.

As I have said numerous times, we do not boast in the manifestations, no matter how they appear. We humble ourselves and boast in Christ. The awesome news was that this woman was brought to a greater place of believing in Christ. In fact, she said it changed her life as she said, "I saw Jesus. I saw Jesus." We can have these transfiguration moments, but we must always point to the Lord. Throughout the life of the mystic Sadhu Sundar Singh, he always pointed people to Jesus, never to himself.

William Branham had the famous picture of the halo over his head. Many of the saints experienced such transfigurations. There are those that said it was a flaming fire, but others said it was a halo.

Whoever desires these types of manifestations can readily enter into them, but it comes through a place of dedication, a place of participation, and a place of sanctification in prayer. I believe that supernatural experiences are usually preceded by a lifetime of seeking God in the secret place of prayer, worship, fasting, and studying the Scriptures.

I remember a manifestation that happened when I was in Bible college. I had been praying and seeking God for six solid months. Six months that included praying to the Lord and fasting. Sometimes, these pursuits of God would last 6-12 hours a day. One particular night, I remember waking up and my whole physical body was, literally, illuminating light. I was in my dorm room and I didn't know where the light was coming from, but it was literally coming out of me. It felt like all my pores were open and wind was blowing through them. Later, I asked the Lord, "Why did I experience that?" I heard Him respond, "Because it's Christ in you, the hope of glory." That experience led me on a journey into Colossians 1:26-27. This was the question that was on my mind, and in my heart: "What is this glory? What does it mean to have Christ in us? What is this illuminating light, this transfiguration glory that is available? What is it?" At that time, I had no concept for any of the things that are presented in this book.

From that one experience, I started asking questions like, "God, is there a glory that is within the believer that we are not even fully tapping into?" And as a result of that, I went on a quest of deeper prayer, and of beholding God, saying, "God, I want to know You." There's a treasure that's in us that's in these earthen vessels, that I've experienced as expressed in Hebrews 1:3. It is the transcendent light of God's glory.

As I conclude, here is my desire: I want to whet your appetite, increasing your desire for more of God. I desire that you understand that there's something more to life than the ordinary Christian life. I want you to ascend to a higher life, filled with supernatural experiences in heavenly realms with the Lord. Don't be content. I believe that God fully intended something greater for you. God wants to fill you with Jesus, so that you are so filled with Him that the glory is manifesting out of you. You can have transfiguration moments like myself and others have had, moments that literally reveal Christ, in all His glory.

I want to see "Christ in us" revealed to this generation. The hope of glory! And I pray that these experiences will glorify God and point people to Christ.

MEET THE AUTHOR

CHARLIE SHAMP is the Co-Founder and President of Destiny Encounters International. He is a sought after international key note speaker. He has been commissioned by Heaven as a Prophet to bring healing and revival in the nations. He has ministered both nationally and internationally with radical demonstrations of faith seeing lives transformed through the power of the Holy Spirit. He resides in Moravian Falls, North Carolina with his wife, Brynn, and their three children.

For more information visit:
DESTINYENCOUNTERS.com

ALSO BY CHARLIE SHAMP

ENDNOTES

1. EXTRACTING THE INVISIBLE

1. https://www.pbs.org/wnet/religionandethics/2008/01/18/january-18-2008-abraham-joshua-heschel/1789/, Accessed January 24, 2020
2. Heb. 11:27
3. Ps. 104, 2 (NIV)
4. https://www.firstthings.com/web-exclusives/2016/10/the-eternity-of-god, Taken from Augustine's book, *Confessions,* Accessed January 28, 2020
5. Matthew 6:10
6. 1 Cor. 14:2
7. https://biblehub.com/commentaries/1_corinthians/14-2.htm, Accessed January 28, 2020
8. https://www.bibletools.org/index.cfm/fuseaction/Topical.show/RTD/CGG/ID/7265/Musterion.htm, Accessed January 28, 2020
9. Ephesians 3:3
10. Romans 12:2
11. Barnes Notes, https://biblehub.com/commentaries/romans/12-2.htm, Accessed January 28, 2020
12. Heb. 12:23
13. Romans 8:5, 6 (NIV)
14. John 3:3, 5
15. John 3:12
16. https://biblehub.com/commentaries/john/3-12.htm, Accessed, January 28, 2020
17. https://wtamu.edu/~cbaird/sq/2014/02/11/why-are-sound-waves-invisible/, Accessed, January 28, 2020
18. https://www.exploratorium.edu/theworld/sonar/sonar.html, Accessed January 28, 2020
19. https://scientificgems.wordpress.com/2015/11/19/pseudoscience-essential-oils/
20. https://purelysimpleorganicliving.com/vibrations-frequencies/, Accessed January 30, 2020
21. Genesis 5:7
22. Ellicott's Commentary, https://biblehub.com/commentaries/genesis/2-7.htm, Accessed January 30, 2020
23. Pulpit Commentary, https://biblehub.com/commentaries/genesis/2-7.htm,, Accessed January 30, 2020

24. Isa. 57:15
25. https://creation.com/the-gospel-in-time-and-space, Accessed January 31, 2020
26. https://www.enotes.com/homework-help/how-sound-light-alike-different-634790, Accessed January 31, 2020
27. https://www.explainthatstuff.com/sound.html, Accessed January 31, 2020
28. http://heavensphysics.com/chapter7/, Accessed January 31, 2020
29. Romans 8:19
30. Gill's Exposition of the Entire Bible, January 31, 2020
31. https://www.gotquestions.org/meaning-of-adamah.html,   Accessed   January 31, 2020
32. 1 Cor 3:16
33. https://www.genome.gov/genetics-glossary/acgt, Accessed January 31, 2020
34. John 1:51, New Living Translation

2. KNOWLEDGE OF GLORY

1. Ephesians 1:17
2. https://www.chabad.org/library/article_cdo/aid/299648/jewish/Daat.htm, Accessed February 2, 2020
3. Hosea 4:6
4. Barnes Notes, https://biblehub.com/commentaries/hosea/4-6.htm, Accessed February 2, 2020
5. Habakkuk 2:14
6. BibleHub https://biblehub.com/library/mathetes/the_epistle_of_mathetes_to_-diognetus/chapter_xii_the_importance_of_knowledge.htm, Accessed February 7, 2020
7. Psalm 19:1, 2, ERV
8. 2 Cor. 4:6
9. Rev. 22:1, 2
10. Isaiah 33:21
11. Psalm 46:4
12. EFBW, https://www.efbw.org/index.php?id=46, Accessed February 4, 2020
13. Psalm 46:4 NASB
14. 1 Cor. 3:9, Amplified Bible
15. Revelation 22:1,2
16. Acts 22:6
17. Benson   Commentary,   https://biblehub.com/commentaries/acts/9-3.htm, Accessed February 4, 2020
18. Isaiah 22:21, 22
19. International Bible Encyclopedia, https://biblehub.com/topical/e/eliakim.htm, Accessed February 5, 2020
20. Bible   History   Online,   https://www.bible-history.com/backd2/sash.html, Accessed February 5, 2020
21. Bible   Study   Tools,   https://www.biblestudytools.com/video/who-was-

melchizedek-and-what-is-his-significance-genesis-14-17-24-hebrews-5-10-7-1.html, Accessed February 5, 2020

22. Bible Study Tools, https://www.biblestudytools.com/lexicons/greek/nas/musterion.html, Accessed February 5, 2020
23. Truth in History, http://truthinhistory.org/tracing-the-steps-of-the-apostle-paul-5.html, Accessed February 5, 2020
24. 1 Corinthians 2:21, 22, NASB
25. Acts 17:28
26. Acts 12:7,8
27. 2 Kings 5:26
28. Barnes Notes, https://biblehub.com/commentaries/2_kings/5-26.htm, Accessed February 6, 2020
29. 1 Cor. 5:3
30. 2 Kings 6:11-12
31. *Studies in Mystical Religion*, Rufus Jones, Macmillan, London, 1923, Pg. Xiv, xv
32. Daniel 5:5, 6
33. Daniel 5:16

3. PANEGYRIS

1. Heb. 12:23
2. Trench's New Testament, https://studybible.info/trench/Church, Accessed February 12, 2020
3. John Gill Commentary, https://www.biblestudytools.com/commentaries/gills-exposition-of-the-bible/hebrews-12-23.html, Accessed February 12, 2020
4. https://biblehub.com/commentaries/acts/2-42.htm, Accessed February 8, 2020
5. https://www.biblestudytools.com/lexicons/greek/nas/basileia.html Accessed February 8, 2020
6. T. Austin-Sparks, The Supernatural Church, http://www,.sermonindex.net/modules/articles/index.php?view=article&aid=21577, Accessed February 8, 2020
7. Matthew 3:2
8. Living stream Ministry, https://www.ministrybooks.org/books.cfm?cid=35, Accessed February 8, 2020
9. Galatians 6:8
10. Galatians 1:16
11. Psalm 133:1,3
12. Eph. 4:16
13. Micah 4:2
14. Psalm 22:22
15. 2 Corinthians 3:18
16. Psalm 89:5
17. Psalm 107:32
18. Psalm 149:1
19. Hebrews 11:40

20. I Corinthians 10:1
21. https://www.biblestudytools.com/commentaries/gills-exposition-of-the-bible/1-corinthians-10-1.html, Accessed February 10, 2020
22. https://biblehub.com/commentaries/hebrews/12-1.htm, Accessed February 10, 2020
23. Ephesians 3:14, 15
24. https://www.spurgeon.org/resource-library/sermons/saints-in-heaven-and-earth-one-family#flipbook/, Accessed February 11, 2020
25. Heb. 4:14
26. Eph. 4:10
27. Hebrews 12:22-24
28. John 14:16
29. Rev. 14:12,13
30. John 8:51,56
31. Rev. 14:14-16

4. TRANSLATION

1. I Cor. 1: 12,13
2. Col. 3:1
3. Jamieson-Faussett-Brown, https://biblehub.com/commentaries/colossians/1-12.htm, Accessed February 16, 2020
4. John 8:12
5. Strongs, https://biblehub.com/greek/3179.htm, February 16, 2020
6. Ellicott's Commentary, https://biblehub.com/commentaries/colossians/1-13.htm, Accessed February 16, 2020
7. Barclays, https://www.preceptaustin.org/colossians_1II-16, Accessed February 16, 2020
8. Gal. 5:25
9. John 8:12
10. Psalm 119:105
11. Luke 4:4
12. Isa. 60:8
13. NASB Lexicon, https://biblehub.com/lexicon/1_corinthians/13-2.htm
14. 2 Cor. 12:2,3
15. https://biblehub.com/commentaries/2_corinthians/12-2.htm, Accessed February 17, 2020
16. Benson Commentary, https://biblehub.com/commentaries/philippians/3-20.htm, Accessed February 19, 2020
17. https://qz.com/866352/scientists-say-your-mind-isnt-confined-to-your-brain-or-even-your-body/, Accessed February 19, 2020
18. Rom. 12:2
19. John 15:7
20. Pulpit Commentary, https://biblehub.com/commentaries/john/15-7.htm, Accessed February 19, 2020

21. Ezra 8:23
22. Acts 16:9, 10, ESV
23. https://biblehub.com/commentaries/acts/16-6.htm, Accessed February 22, 2020
24. Heb. 4:12
25. Rev. 4:1
26. Jeremiah 23:18, NASB
27. Isaiah 40:29, 31

5. TRANS-RELOCATION

1. 2 Cor. 4:18
2. https://www.dictionary.com/browse/super-
3. John Nepil, https://thosecatholicmen.com/articles/767/ , Accessed February 22, 2020
4. https://priscillastuckey.com/nature-spirit/what-is-natural-what-is-supernatural/, Accessed February 22, 2020
5. https://thosecatholicmen.com/articles/767/, Accessed February 22, 2020
6. Romans 8:2
7. https://www.biblestudytools.com/commentaries/gills-exposition-of-the-bible/romans-8-2.html, Accessed February 23, 2020
8. Ezekiel 8:3
9. Lev. 4:6
10. *The Heavenly Man,* Brother Yun, Paul Hattaway (Oxford, England: Monarch Books, 2002) 22, 23
11. Acts 8:39
12. Red Letter Christians, https://www.redletterchristians.org/the-expanding-kingdom-philip-the-ethiopian-eunuch/, Accessed February 24, 2020
13. Benson Commentary, https://biblehub.com/commentaries/acts/8-39.htm, Accessed February 26, 2020
14. Luke 4:18
15. Hebrews 2:10
16. Romans 18:11
17. https://www.studylight.org/commentaries/tpc/1-kings-18.html, Accessed February 24, 2020
18. John 6:16-21
19. MacLaren's Exposition, https://biblehub.com/commentaries/john/6-19.htm, Accessed February 25, 2020
20. Mark 7:10
21. Matthew 10:11
22. Weymouth New Testament, 2 Timothy 1:7
23. Revelation 2:1-5
24. Matthew 22:36-40
25. Come Thou Fount of Every Blessing, https://www.hymnal.net/en/hymn/h/319, Accessed February 25, 2020

26. Henri Nouwen, https://henrinouwen.org/meditation/doing-love/, Accessed February 26, 2020

6. BILOCATION

1. https://www.stcubyduloe.org.uk/welcome-to-st-cuby-in-duloe/sermons/, Accessed February 28, 2020
2. https://bradstrait.com/2011/08/22/what-is-a-christian-mystic/, Accessed February 28, 2020
3. https://www.patheos.com/blogs/carlmccolman/2014/07/the-hidden-tradition-of-christian-mysticism-2/, Accessed February 29, 2020
4. https://spiritualdirection.com/2018/11/05/union-with-god, Accessed February 29, 2020
5. http://spacecollective.org/redacted?3930/The-Five-Steps-to-Mysticism, Accessed February 29, 2020
6. Exodus 3:7
7. https://stephenbarkley.com/2019/02/11/the-prophetic-imagination-walter-brueggemann/, Accessed March 1, 2020
8. https://www.christianitytoday.com/history/people/innertravelers/catherine-of-siena.html, Accessed March 1, 2020
9. https://mollylannonkenny.org/howard-thurman-jesus-disinherited-first-published-1949-personal-reflection/, Accessed March 1, 2020
10. https://progressivechristianity.org/resources/mysticism-and-social-action-the-spirituality-of-howard-thurman/#_ftn2, Accessed March 1, 2020
11. Howard Thurman, *Mysticism and Social Action, Kindle location, 249-251*
12. https://www.padrepio.catholicwebservices.com/ENGLISH/Bilo.htm, Accessed March 3, 2020
13. https://aleteia.org/2019/09/23/how-padre-pio-stopped-allied-forces-from-bombing-his-monastery-during-wwii/, Accessed March 3, 2020
14. https://catholicmystics.blogspot.com/p/bilocation-bilocation-is-phenomenon-in.html, Accessed March 1, 2020
15. Eph. 2:6
16. https://biblehub.com/commentaries/ephesians/2-6.htm (all are located in this location), Accessed March 1, 2020
17. https://www.biblestudytools.com/lexicons/greek/kjv/epouranios.html, Accessed March 1, 2020
18. Psalm 8
19. Genesis 1:28
20. Romans 8:19
21. https://biblehub.com/commentaries/romans/8-19.htm, Expositor's Greek New Testament, Accessed March 1, 2020
22. https://biblehub.com/commentaries/romans/8-19.htm, Matthew Poole's Commentary, Accessed March 1, 2020
23. https://catholicmystics.blogspot.com/p/bilocation-bilocation-is-phenomenon-in.html, Accessed March 2, 2020

24. https://www.churchmilitant.com/news/article/legend-of-the-lady-in-blue-presented-to-vatican, Accessed March 2, 2020
25. https://www.churchmilitant.com/news/article/legend-of-the-lady-in-blue-presented-to-vatican, March 2, 2020
26. Isaiah 40:22
27. https://biblehub.com/commentaries/isaiah/40-22.htm, Accessed March 2, 2020
28. Daryl Coley, https://genius.com/Daryl-coley-beyond-the-veil-lyrics, Accessed March 2, 2020

7. GENETICAL TRANSFIGURATIONS, PART ONE

1. Psalm 139:14
2. https://www.beliefnet.com/news/science-religion/2006/08/god-is-not-threatened-by-our-scientific-adventures.aspx. Accessed March 6, 2020
3. 1 Corinthians 2:11-13, NASB
4. The Epistle of Polycarp to the Philippians, https://www.christian-history.org/polycarps-philippian-epistle.html, Accessed March 6, 2020
5. Cross, F. L., ed. *The Oxford Dictionary of the Christian Church* (New York: Oxford University Press, 2005)
6. Against Heresies, Book 5, preface, https://www.taize.fr/en_article6431.html, Accessed March 6, 2020
7. John 1:14
8. Col. 1:27
9. Gal. 3:26
10. Pulpit Commentary, https://biblehub.com/commentaries/john/1-14.htm, Accessed March 6, 2020
11. Irenaeus, https://www.crossroadsinitiative.com/media/articles/man-fully-alive-is-the-glory-of-god-st-irenaeus/, Accessed March 6, 2020
12. 2 Cor. 3:18
13. Rom. 8:29
14. Expositor's Greek New Testament, https://biblehub.com/commentaries/2_corinthians/3-18.htm, Accessed March 6, 2020
15. MacLaren/s Exposition, https://biblehub.com/commentaries/2_corinthians/3-18.htm, Accessed March 6, 2020
16. Gen. 4:16, 17
17. https://billrandles.wordpress.com/2012/12/19/why-cain-built-a-city-genesis-4-pt-8/, Accessed, March 6, 2020
18. Gen. 12:1
19. Heb. 11:10
20. Gen. 3:15
21. https://askabiologist.asu.edu/dna-shape-and-structure, Accessed March 7, 2020
22. Popular Science https://www.popsci.com/new-dna-shape/ March 9, 2020
23. https://www.biblestudytools.com/lexicons/greek/nas/logos.html, Accessed March 7, 2020
24. 1 Cor. 2:16

25. Gen. 1:26

26. Barnes Notes, https://biblehub.com/commentaries/genesis/1-26.htm, March 7, 2020

27. https://steemit.com/christian-trail/@livingwaters/in-the-beginning-god-said-and-the-law-of-vibration, Accessed March 7, 2020

28. Rev. 13:8

29. https://biblehub.com/commentaries/revelation/13-8.htm, Accessed March 7, 2020

30. Gen. 2:7

31. Ellicott's Commentary, https://biblehub.com/commentaries/genesis/2-7.htm, Accessed March 7, 2020

32. Acts 3:21

33. 1 Cor. 15:45-49

34. Bengel's Gnomon, https://biblehub.com/commentaries/1_corinthians/15-49.htm, Accessed March 8, 2020

35. Isaiah 14:12, 14

36. I Kings 8:27

37. 1 Cor. 6:19, 20

38. 2 Peter 1:3, 4

39. Alexander Mclaren, https://biblehub.com/commentaries/2_peter/1-4.htm, March 8, 2020

40. http://ww1.antiochian.org/content/theosis-partaking-divine-nature, March 9, 2020

41. John 17:20, 21

42. http://www.tertullian.org/fathers/cyril_on_john_01_book1.htm, March 9, 2020

43. Theosis Part II: YouTube, Frederica Matthews-Green

44. http://ww1.antiochian.org/content/theosis-partaking-divine-nature, March 13, 2020

45. https://www.preceptaustin.org/search/node?keys=energizing, Accessed March 9, 2020

46. https://orthodoxword.wordpress.com/2010/03/02/vladimir-lossky-on-the-essence-and-energies-of-god, Accessed March 9, 2020

47. https://biblehub.com/commentaries/acts/17-28.htm, Accessed March 9, 2020

48. https://hermeneutics.stackexchange.com/questions/8554/in-2-peter-14-what-does-peter-mean-by-partakers-of-the-divine-nature, March 9, 2020

49. Ibid

50. Book of Jasher 1:27

51. Luke 1:34,35

52. https://en.wikipedia.org/wiki/Incarnation_(Christianity)#Nicene_Creed, Accessed March 10, 2020

53. https://en.wikipedia.org/wiki/Docetism, Accessed March 10, 2020

54. Acts 10:39,40

55. Hebrews 1:1,2

56. Matthew 18:20

57. https://ourrabbijesus.com/articles/where-two-or-three-are-gathered-in-context/, March 10, 2020

58. John 3:3
59. Luke 17:20,21

8. GENETIC TRANSFIGURATIONS, PART TWO

1. Pulpit Commentary, https://biblehub.com/commentaries/genesis/28-12.htm, Accessed March 10, 2020
2. Exodus 34:33
3. https://www.breadforbeggars.com/2019/03/the-horns-of-moses-and-the-veiled-glory-of-jesus/, March 10, 2020
4. http://www.hebroots.org/hebrootsarchive/9901/9901_q.html, March 11, 2020
5. https://www.bibletools.org/index.cfm/fuseaction/Topical.show/RTD/cgg/ID/388/Nimrod.htm, March 11, 2020
6. Isaiah 14:13,14
7. 1 Peter 1:23
8. 2 Timothy 2:15
9. https://biblehub.com/commentaries/1_peter/1-10.htm, March 11, 2020
10. Daniel 9:25
11. 1 Peter 1:23
12. 1 John 3:9
13. Mark 11:24
14. Proverbs 13:12
15. Jude 1:20
16. https://www.oca.org/orthodoxy/the-orthodox-faith/spirituality/prayer-fasting-and-almsgiving/prayer-in-the-spirit, March 11, 2020
17. Psalms 63:6
18. Hebrews 10:19, 22
19. Psalm 84:7
20. https://www.studylight.org/commentary/psalms/84-7.html, March 11, 2020
21. 1 Cor. 10:16
22. John 6:53, 54
23. http://www.therealpresence.org/eucharst/father/a5.html#ignatius, March 12, 2020
24. Ibid
25. Ibid
26. Ibid
27. Ibid
28. Ibid
29. https://en.wikipedia.org/wiki/Transubstantiation#cite_note-1, March 12, 2020
30. https://blessedsacrament.com/the-eucharist-in-eastern-orthodoxy/, March 12, 2020
31. Eph. 2:6
32. https://joshbrisby.blogspot.com/2006/01/mystery-of-lords-supper.html, March 12, 2020
33. John 6:51

34. Psalm 110:1-4
35. Ephesians 5:30

9. TRANSFIGURATION

1. Luke 9:28,29
2. E.M. Bounds, http://articles.ochristian.com/article12079.shtml, March 14, 2020
3. http://daughterofthechurch.weebly.com/visions-teresa-avila.html, Accessed March 14, 2020
4. https://www.ccel.org/ccel/rolle/fire.html, Accessed March 14, 2020
5. http://people.bu.edu/dklepper/RN413/rolle.html, Accessed March 14, 2020
6. John 14:12
7. 2 Cor. 3:10, 11, Amplified Bible
8. Hebrews 6:18-20
9. Luke:24:24-26
10. Revelation 1:12-17
11. Revelation 5:6
12. 2 Cor. 4:5,6
13. https://biblehub.com/commentaries/2_corinthians/4-6.htm, Accessed March 15, 2020
14. Heb. 1:3, AMP
15. John 4:34
16. 2 Corinthians 4:7
17. Hebrews 1:3

Made in the USA
Middletown, DE
17 September 2020

19401813R00115